ALL ABOUT ALGAE

Exploring Algology or Phycology

A Comprehensive Guide to Algae and their Significance

A Compendium from BS 101 to PHD 900

Written by

David Alan Binder

ISBN: 978-93-58048-50-6
eISBN: 978-93-58048-51-3

©Author

Publisher: Pharos Books (P) Ltd.
Plot No.-55, Main Mother Dairy Road
Pandav Nagar, East Delhi-110092
Phone: 011-40395855, +4049916623
WhatsApp: +91 8368220032
E-mail: sales@pharosbooks.in
Website: www.pharosbooks.in
First Edition: 2023

ALL ABOUT ALGAE
By David Alan Binder

A captivating and informative collection, this scholarly compendium textbook blends education and entertainment seamlessly. Delving into the fascinating realm of Algology or Phycology, the study of algae, it offers an intriguing subject for exploration. The book is divided into various levels, starting from Bachelor's 101 and progressing all the way to Doctorate 900, while maintaining a remarkably accessible writing style.

Algae, the focus of this compendium, encompasses a rich array of essential components: chlorophyll, nutrients, oxygen, carbon, nitrogen, carbohydrates, lipids, and nucleic acids. It serves as the foundation for many fundamental biological processes. However, its significance extends far beyond the basics, as algae hold the potential to address a wide range of challenges.

In the realm of sustenance, algae emerge as a potential panacea for hunger. Its application as food stretches further into realms such as space missions, medicine, and biofuels. Moreover, the versatile nature of algae finds expression in art, vegan diets, health, makeup, fertilizer, paper recycling, music, energy production, pharmaceuticals, and even as a superior fuel source for athletes.

A comprehensive, engaging and thought-provoking journey into the captivating world of algae. It highlights not only its scientific importance but also its numerous practical applications across various domains, inviting readers to appreciate the true potential of this remarkable organism.

PREFACE

Marie C. and other invaluable contributors, who prefer to remain anonymous, have provided exceptional cooperation, expertise, advice, counselling, and answers to numerous questions throughout this writing project. A vast array of researchers and assistants have contributed to this text. Acknowledgements to SDSU (my alma mater) Department of Biology plus numerous graduate and undergraduate students has made this book a shining example and an exceptional compendium.

As an author and writer, I have facilitated the gathering of knowledge from this remarkable team. One of the resources available to me is the Sandia National Laboratories, located in close proximity, where they are conducting tests on one of California's largest and most polluted lakes. Their objective is to determine if this lake can be transformed into a productive and profitable space. Just a short distance, less than half an hour north of my location, lies Southern California's Salton Sea, spanning 350 square miles. Unfortunately, this area is plagued by well-documented issues related to high levels of nitrogen and phosphorus from agricultural runoff. Algae thrive on these elements, which not only causes environmental problems but also presents an opportunity for finding solutions.

The Sandia National Laboratories are working diligently to harness algae's remarkable ability to grow abundantly. Their goal is to utilize this property to clean up pollutants and mitigate harmful algae blooms in the Salton Sea, all while creating a renewable source of fuel. Through Sandia Labs' patented fermentation process, algae can be easily converted into fuels and chemicals.

According to the Department of Energy's Bioenergy Technology Office (BETO), it is estimated that the United States can produce at least 1 billion tons of feedstocks for biofuels annually. Achieving this target would yield positive social, economic, and environmental impacts. Notably, algae stand out among these feedstocks due to its unique ability to grow exponentially, doubling in quantity each day under favourable conditions.

Extensive exploration around the Salton Sea has provided insights into the numerous manifestations of its problems and challenges. However, amidst these issues, there are glimmers of hope and promise reflected in the sea, as well as in the abundant sunshine that graces the region for 309 days each year. This characteristic alone positions the area as an ideal production hub for heat, attracting winter visitors, cultivating crops, and fostering various industries with great potential and prospects.

*In heartfelt dedication, this book is lovingly dedicated to
Katherine Anne (Malone) Binder, celebrating the enduring love,
prosperity, and shared journey between us.*

We take great pride in and hold deep love for our family.

*To Mahip Bhatia, Neeharika Lodhi and Pharos Books Private Limited for
providing the Printing Services, Publishing Services, Cover Page Design.*

Thanks to all those who played a role in bringing this book to the light of day.

To all my readers and followers.

CONTENTS

INTRODUCTION

Algology, also known as phycology, is the study of algae, a diverse group of photosynthetic organisms that play important roles in ecosystems around the world. Despite their significance, algae are often overlooked in popular discussions of biology, and many people are unaware of their ecological, economic, and cultural importance.

Exploring Algology: A Comprehensive Guide to Algae and their Significance is a book that aims to fill this gap in knowledge. This book provides a comprehensive overview of algae and their significance, covering topics such as their classification, physiology, ecology, and biotechnology applications.

Welcome to the captivating world of phycology, a field of study that unravels the mysteries of algae and their profound significance in the realm of biology. From the microscopic to the macroscopic, algae exist in astonishing diversity and exert a remarkable influence on our planet's ecosystems. In this comprehensive guide, we invite you to embark on a journey through the captivating world of algae, uncovering their hidden wonders and unravelling their role in shaping the natural world.

Algology, also known as phycology, is the scientific study of algae. Algae, often referred to as "the plants of the sea," are a group of diverse and ubiquitous organisms that thrive in a variety of environments, ranging from freshwater to marine habitats, and even on land. Although they are not true plants, algae have contributed significantly to our understanding of fundamental biological processes and have profound ecological implications.

This book serves as a comprehensive resource, shedding light on the captivating world of algae and elucidating their significance in the study of biology. Its contents encompass a wide array of topics, ranging from the fundamental aspects of algal biology to their ecological roles and applications in various fields.

The book begins by laying the foundation of algology, offering a comprehensive explanation of what algae are, their evolutionary history, and their classification into different taxonomic groups. It explores the unique characteristics of various algal groups, including diatoms, green algae, red algae, brown algae, and cyanobacteria, delving into their morphology, physiology, and reproduction strategies.

As we venture deeper into the book, we explore the ecological significance of algae, highlighting their crucial roles in nutrient cycling, oxygen production, and their intricate relationships with other organisms in aquatic ecosystems. We also delve into the fascinating phenomenon of harmful algal blooms, uncovering the environmental and human health impacts they pose and the strategies employed to manage and mitigate their effects.

Moreover, this comprehensive guide delves into the applications of algae in diverse fields, ranging from biotechnology and biofuels to food production and wastewater treatment. We explore the potential of algae as sustainable resources, their role in carbon sequestration, and their use in the production of pharmaceuticals and nutraceuticals. Please note that a nutraceutical product may be defined as a substance, which has physiological benefits or provides protection against chronic disease.

Throughout the book, we present engaging case studies, captivating anecdotes, and stunning visuals to bring the world of algae to life, making it accessible and intriguing for both beginners and seasoned enthusiasts alike. Our goal is to provide a holistic understanding of algology, empowering readers to appreciate the beauty and significance of algae while recognizing their immense impact on the functioning of our planet.

Whether you are a student, a researcher, a nature enthusiast, or simply curious about the wonders of the natural world, this book will serve as your comprehensive guide to phycology. Its carefully structured chapters and accessible language ensure that readers of all backgrounds can grasp the intricacies of algae and their significance.

As you delve into the pages of this book, you will find a wealth of knowledge awaiting you. Explore the incredible diversity of algae, from the microscopic unicellular species to the majestic kelp forests. Gain insight into the various habitats they inhabit, from freshwater lakes and rivers to the vast expanses of the ocean. Discover how their adaptations and abilities have allowed them to thrive in such diverse environments.

Throughout the book, we provide vivid descriptions and illustrations of the remarkable forms and colours that algae take, showcasing their beauty and captivating allure. You will learn about the intricate structures of diatoms, the elegant filaments of green algae, the delicate branches of red algae, and the towering fronds of brown algae. Witness the mesmerizing phenomenon of bioluminescent algae and the breathtaking patterns they create in the night.

Furthermore, this guide emphasizes the ecological importance of algae. Understand their role as primary producers, generating oxygen through photosynthesis and forming the foundation of food chains in aquatic ecosystems. Discover their crucial symbiotic relationships with coral reefs and their influence on the health and stability of marine environments. Gain insight into the fascinating interactions between algae and other organisms, including animals, bacteria, and fungi.

As you progress through the book, you will encounter discussions on the various research methodologies employed in algology, including laboratory techniques, microscopy, and molecular analysis. We provide guidance on how to collect and study algae, empowering readers to embark on their own explorations and investigations.

In addition to their ecological significance, algae hold tremendous potential for human applications. Delve into the field of algal biotechnology, where researchers harness the unique properties of algae for the production of biofuels, pharmaceuticals, and valuable compounds. Discover the promising advancements in algae-based wastewater treatment, agricultural fertilizers, and even the production of sustainable materials.

By the time you reach the final pages of this book, you will have gained a profound appreciation for the immense significance of algae in the study of biology and the functioning of our planet. You will recognize their influence on global ecosystems, their aesthetic beauty, and the vast array of applications they offer to human society.

Let us explore together, marvelling at their resilience, diversity, and profound impact on the biological tapestry of life. This comprehensive guide will empower you with knowledge, ignite your curiosity, and unveil the hidden wonders that lie beneath the surface of our aquatic environments.

CHAPTER 1

Algae in History and Culture

Algae have been an important part of human history and culture for thousands of years. Throughout history, different cultures around the world have recognized the value of algae for their various properties, including their nutritional, medicinal, and artistic uses. This chapter explores the historical use of algae in food, medicine, and art, as well as the significance of algae in different cultures around the world.

Historical use of algae in food, medicine, and art:

Algae have been used as a source of food for thousands of years. In China, for example, seaweed has been consumed for over 2,000 years and is an important ingredient in many traditional dishes (Burrows, 1991). In Japan, seaweed is used in a variety of dishes, including sushi, miso soup, and nori (dried seaweed) snacks (Huisman, 2018; Round, Chapman, & Maberly, 2014). Similarly, in coastal areas of Scotland and Ireland, seaweed has been an important part of the local diet for centuries (Graham, Graham, & Wilcox, 2009).

Algae have also been used for medicinal purposes in many cultures. In traditional Chinese medicine, seaweed is used to treat a variety of ailments, including thyroid disorders, high blood pressure, and inflammation (Huisman, 2018). In other parts of the world, algae have been used to treat wounds, stomach disorders, and skin diseases (Graham et al., 2009; Raven, 2013).

In addition to their practical uses, algae have also been used for artistic purposes. For example, in medieval Europe, algae were used to make pigments for paints and dyes (Huisman, 2018). In Japan, seaweed has been used in traditional papermaking (Huisman, 2018), while in China, algae have been used to make ink for calligraphy (Burrows, 1991).

The significance of algae in different cultures around the world:

In many cultures, algae have played important symbolic and spiritual roles. In ancient Egypt, for example, blue-green algae were believed to be the source of life and were associated with the god Osiris (Raven, 2013). In Japan, seaweed has been used in Shinto rituals as a symbol of purity and longevity (Huisman, 2018).

Algae have also been used in traditional folk medicine and beliefs. In some African cultures, for example, algae are used in rituals to protect against evil spirits (Graham et al., 2009). In Hawaii, seaweed is used in traditional healing practices and is believed to have spiritual and medicinal properties (Huisman, 2018).

India has a rich history of using algae for various purposes. In traditional Ayurvedic medicine, algae such as Spirulina and Chlorella have been used to treat a variety of ailments, including digestive disorders, anaemia, and allergies (Graham et al., 2009; Huisman, 2018). These algae are also considered to have detoxifying properties and are used in detoxification therapies (Watanabe & Hattori, 2001).

In addition to their medicinal uses, algae have also been used as a source of food in India for centuries. In coastal areas, seaweed is commonly used in dishes such as sambar, a lentil soup, and kichadi, a rice and lentil dish (Huisman, 2018). Algae such as spirulina and chlorella are also used as dietary supplements and are believed to provide a range of health benefits (Graham et al., 2009).

The significance of algae in cultures of India:

Algae have also played important cultural roles in India. Algae is an important part of Indian art and culture. In the southern Indian state of Tamil Nadu, for example, women decorate their homes with intricate patterns made from rice flour and seaweed during the Pongal festival, a harvest festival celebrated in January (Huisman, 2018).

The historical use of algae in India highlights their importance in traditional medicine, food, and culture. Algae have played important spiritual and cultural roles in Hinduism, and their use in traditional dishes and art demonstrates their significance in everyday life (Huisman, 2018). Understanding the cultural significance of algae in India can help us appreciate their value and importance in the natural world.

SECTION 1: HISTORICAL USE OF ALGAE IN FOOD, MEDICINE, AND ART

Throughout human history, algae have played a significant role in various aspects of human life, including food, medicine, and art. This chapter explores the historical use of algae and uncovers their remarkable contributions to these domains.

1.1 ALGAE AS A SOURCE OF FOOD

Algae have been utilized as a source of sustenance by different cultures for centuries. In ancient civilizations such as China, Japan, and the indigenous peoples of the Americas, seaweed and other edible algae were incorporated into their diets. These marine plants provided valuable nutrients, including proteins, vitamins, and minerals, supplementing traditional food sources. The cultivation and consumption of algae for food continue to this day, with seaweeds finding their way into modern cuisine as nutritious and flavorful ingredients.

1.2 ALGAE IN TRADITIONAL MEDICINE

The therapeutic properties of algae have been recognized and harnessed by traditional medical practices across various cultures. In ancient Egypt, for example, the use of blue-green algae (cyanobacteria) in medicinal preparations was documented. Indigenous cultures in Africa, Asia, and the Americas employed algae in remedies for various ailments, ranging from digestive disorders to skin conditions. The antimicrobial, anti-inflammatory, and antioxidant properties of certain algae species made them valuable additions to traditional pharmacopoeias.

1.3 ALGAE IN ART AND CULTURE

Algae have also left an indelible mark on the world of art and culture. From ancient times to the present day, artists have drawn inspiration from the vibrant colours, intricate patterns, and unique forms of algae. In Japanese culture, the art of Gyotaku involved creating prints of fish using ink made from seaweed. In European art, seaweed motifs were prevalent in decorative arts and architecture during the Victorian era. Today, contemporary artists continue to explore the aesthetic appeal of algae, integrating them into various artistic expressions.

SECTION 2: THE SIGNIFICANCE OF ALGAE IN DIFFERENT CULTURES AROUND THE WORLD

2.1 ALGAE IN ASIAN CULTURES

Algae hold great cultural significance in many Asian countries. In Japan, the tradition of nori farming dates back centuries, with seaweed cultivation playing a central role in coastal communities. Nori, a type of red algae, is an essential ingredient in sushi and other Japanese dishes. Similarly, China has a long history of using algae in traditional medicine and cuisine. The vibrant green Spirulina, a type of cyanobacteria, is highly valued for its nutritional properties and is consumed as a dietary supplement.

2.2 ALGAE IN INDIGENOUS CULTURES

Indigenous peoples around the world have developed a deep connection with algae, recognizing their importance in their cultural and ecological landscapes. For instance, the Maori of New Zealand consider edible seaweeds a taonga (treasure) and an essential part of their diet. Indigenous communities in coastal regions of North America, such as the Haida and the Tlingit, have incorporated seaweeds into their traditional dishes, acknowledging their nutritional value and cultural heritage.

In Western cultures, the significance of algae has evolved over time. In ancient Greece, algae were described by philosophers and naturalists, contributing to early botanical knowledge. In the Victorian era, seaweed collecting became a popular recreational activity for seaside tourists, leading to the creation of elaborate albums showcasing pressed seaweeds. Today, the ecological and scientific importance of algae is widely recognized, driving research and conservation efforts.

By exploring the historical use of algae in food, medicine, and art, as well as their cultural significance around the world, we gain a deeper understanding of the profound influence these organisms have had on human societies throughout history. In the subsequent chapters,

We will delve further into the biology, ecology, and applications of algae, building upon this foundation of historical and cultural context.

Chapter 1 sets the stage for our exploration of algae by highlighting their multifaceted roles in human civilization. By examining their use as a source of food and medicine, we uncover the wisdom and ingenuity of ancient cultures that recognized the value of these organisms long before modern scientific understanding. Additionally, we appreciate the artistic inspiration that algae have provided to artists across different eras and cultures, underscoring their aesthetic allure.

Moreover, we recognize that algae hold cultural significance in various regions of the world. From Asia, where seaweed cultivation has been ingrained in traditional practices and cuisine, to indigenous communities that have deep-rooted connections with algae, we discover the profound respect and reverence these organisms have commanded.

As we journey through the subsequent chapters, we will deepen our understanding of the biology and ecology of algae, exploring their diverse forms, intricate life cycles, and ecological roles. We will also investigate the applications of algae in modern society, including their potential as sustainable food sources, their contribution to pharmaceuticals and biotechnology, and their impact on environmental conservation.

Continue to unravel the captivating world of algae, bridging the gap between historical and cultural perspectives and cutting-edge scientific advancements. By exploring the significance of algae in various realms, we gain a holistic perspective on these remarkable organisms and their contributions to the tapestry of human existence. Let us embark on this comprehensive journey, guided by curiosity and a desire to uncover the hidden wonders of algae.

Conclusion:

Overall, algae have played a significant role in human history and culture for thousands of years. From their use as a source of food and medicine to their role in art and spirituality, algae have been an important part of human life around the world. Understanding the historical significance of algae can help us appreciate their value and importance in the natural world.

CHAPTER 2

Algae Classification and Diversity

Algae are a diverse group of photosynthetic organisms that can be found in a wide range of habitats, including freshwater, saltwater, soil, and symbiotically with other organisms. They are classified based on their morphology, biochemistry, and genetics.

Classification of Algae Based on Morphology

Algae can be classified based on their morphology, including the structure and shape of their cells, as well as their overall appearance. The major morphological characteristics used in the classification of algae include cell wall composition, pigmentation, and cell structure (Graham et al., 2009; Huisman, 2018; Round et al., 2014).

Classification of Algae Based on Biochemistry

Algae can also be classified based on their biochemistry, including the types of pigments they contain, the type of photosynthesis they undergo, and the nature of their energy storage molecules. The major biochemical characteristics used in the classification of algae include photosynthetic pigments, photosynthetic pathways, and energy storage molecules (Graham et al., 2009; Huisman, 2018; Larkum et al., 2012; Raven, 2013).

Classification of Algae Based on Genetics

Algae can also be classified based on their genetics, including the genetic sequences of their DNA and RNA. The major genetic characteristics used in the classification of algae include ribosomal RNA sequences and chloroplast genome sequences (Graham et al., 2009; Guiry & Guiry, 2021; Huisman, 2018; Van der Meer, 2015; Watanabe & Hattori, 2001).

Overview of the Different Groups of Algae and their Disti guishing Characteristics

Algae can be classified into several different groups, each with its own distinguishing characteristics. The major groups of algae include Cyanobacteria, Chlorophyta, Rhodophyta, Phaeophyta, Bacillariophyta, Dinophyta, Euglenophyta, and Charophyta (Burrows, 1991; Graham et al., 2009; Guiry & Guiry, 2021; Huisman, 2018; Larkum et al., 2012; Raven, 2013; Round et al., 2014; Stewart & Fitzgerald, 1980).

Algae Classification and Diversity

Algae, a diverse group of photosynthetic organisms, exhibit a remarkable array of forms, adaptations, and ecological roles. In this chapter, we delve into the classification and diversity of algae, exploring the various criteria used to categorize them and providing an overview of the different groups and their distinguishing characteristics.

SECTION 1: CLASSIFICATION OF ALGAE

1.1 MORPHOLOGICAL CLASSIFICATION

Algae can be classified based on their morphology, which encompasses their overall form, cellular structure, and reproductive strategies. This classification system takes into account features such as cell organization (unicellular, colonial, or multicellular), cell shape (round, filamentous, or branched), presence or absence of specialized structures (flagella, chloroplasts, holdfasts), and modes of reproduction (sexual or asexual). Morphological classification provides a convenient way to identify and differentiate algae based on visible characteristics.

1.2 BIOCHEMICAL CLASSIFICATION

Another approach to classifying algae is based on their biochemical composition. Algae produce a wide range of pigments, including chlorophylls, carotenoids, and phycobilins, which contribute to their distinctive colours. These pigments can be analyzed and used to classify algae into different groups. Additionally, the presence of unique cell wall components, such as cellulose, silica, or carrageenan, further aids in their classification. Biochemical classification provides insights into the metabolic and physiological characteristics of algae.

1.3 GENETIC CLASSIFICATION

With the advent of molecular techniques, genetic information has become crucial in classifying algae. Genetic classification is based on the analysis of their DNA sequences, which allows for a more accurate understanding of their evolutionary relationships. Through genetic analysis, scientists can uncover the genetic diversity within and among algal groups, shedding light on their evolutionary history and phylogenetic relationships. This approach has led to significant revisions in the classification of algae and has provided insights into their evolutionary origins.

SECTION 2 OVERVIEW OF ALGAL GROUPS

2.1 CYANOBACTERIA (BLUE-GREEN ALGAE)

Cyanobacteria, often referred to as blue-green algae, are prokaryotic organisms that possess chlorophyll and other pigments. They are typically unicellular or filamentous and can be found in a wide range of habitats, including freshwater, marine environments, and terrestrial ecosystems. Cyanobacteria play crucial roles in oxygen production, nitrogen fixation, and primary production, and some species form symbiotic relationships with plants or animals.

2.2 MICROALGAE (DIATOMS, DINOFLAGELLATES, AND OTHERS)

Microalgae encompass a diverse group of eukaryotic organisms that include diatoms, dinoflagellates, and other unicellular or colonial forms. Diatoms, characterized by their intricate silica cell walls, are abundant in marine and freshwater environments and play a significant role in global carbon cycling. Dinoflagellates are known for their diverse shapes, two flagella, and some species are responsible for harmful algal blooms and bioluminescence.

2.3 GREEN ALGAE

Green algae, which include both unicellular and multicellular forms, are characterized by their chlorophyll a and b pigments, as well as their storage of starch as a carbohydrate reserve. They can be found in various habitats, from freshwater to marine environments, and even in symbiotic associations with other organisms. Green algae exhibit a wide range of forms, from single-celled Chlamydomonas to complex multicellular species like Ulva (sea lettuce).

2.4 RED ALGAE

Red algae are primarily marine organisms that possess unique pigments called phycobilins, which give them their characteristic red colour. They are predominantly multicellular, ranging from filamentous forms to more complex, leafy structures. Red algae play significant roles in marine ecosystems, forming important components of coral reefs and contributing to calcium carbonate deposition. They are also utilized for various purposes, such as food additives (e.g., agar and carrageenan) and biomedical applications.

2.5 BROWN ALGAE

Brown algae are predominantly marine organisms known for their characteristic brown colour, which is due to the presence of fucoxanthin pigments. They exhibit a wide range of forms, from small filamentous species to large, structurally complex seaweeds such as kelp. Brown algae are ecologically important, providing habitats for numerous marine organisms and contributing to coastal ecosystems. They are also utilized commercially for food, pharmaceuticals, and agricultural applications.

SECTION 3: UNDERSTANDING ALGAE DIVERSITY

Algae exhibit an incredible diversity of forms, adaptations, and ecological roles. From the microscopic cyanobacteria to the towering kelp forests, algae have conquered nearly every habitat on Earth. Their classification based on morphology, biochemistry, and genetics provides a framework for understanding and organizing this diversity.

By studying the different groups of algae, we gain insights into their unique characteristics and evolutionary relationships. We can appreciate their contributions to various ecosystems, from primary production and nutrient cycling to providing habitats and serving as important resources for human society.

In the subsequent chapters, we will delve deeper into the biology and ecology of each algal group, exploring their physiology, life cycles, ecological interactions, and applications. By unravelling the intricacies of algae, we aim to foster a comprehensive understanding of these fascinating organisms and their significance in the natural world.

The exploration of the rich tapestry of algal diversity, uncovering the secrets of their evolutionary history, ecological roles, and the remarkable adaptations that have allowed them to thrive in diverse environments. Together, let us delve into the captivating world of algae and unravel the mysteries they hold.

In conclusion, algae are a diverse group of photosynthetic organisms that can be classified based on their morphology, biochemistry, and genetics. The major groups of algae include cyanobacteria, chlorophyta, rhodophyta, phaeophyta, bacillariophyta, dinophyta, euglenophyta, and charophyta. Each group has its own unique characteristics and plays an important role in different ecosystems. Understanding the classification and diversity of algae is essential for understanding their ecological and economic importance.

CHAPTER 3

Algae Physiology and Ecology

Algae are a diverse group of aquatic organisms that play critical roles in the functioning of ecosystems worldwide. Their physiological and ecological characteristics are shaped by their evolutionary history and environmental conditions, such as temperature, light, nutrient availability, and water chemistry. In this chapter, we will provide an overview of the physiology and ecology of algae, discuss the role of algae in various ecosystems, and highlight the importance of algae in the global carbon cycle and oxygen production.

Overview of the Physiology and Ecology of Algae

Algae are photosynthetic organisms that use chlorophyll and other pigments to convert light energy into chemical energy through photosynthesis. They have different morphologies, from unicellular to multicellular forms, and can be found in a range of aquatic habitats, from freshwater ponds and streams to the open ocean. Algae are typically classified into six groups based on their pigmentation and cell structure: Chlorophyta (green algae), Rhodophyta (red algae), Phaeophyta (brown algae), Bacillariophyta (diatoms), Dinophyta (dinoflagellates), and Cyanobacteria (blue-green algae) (Burrows, 1991; Graham et al., 2009; Guiry & Guiry, 2021; Huisman, 2018; Larkum et al., 2012; Raven, 2013; Round et al., 2014; Stewart & Fitzgerald, 1980).

Algae have unique physiological adaptations that allow them to survive and thrive in a wide range of environmental conditions. For example, some algae can change their pigment composition and adjust their photosynthetic machinery to different light spectra, allowing them to photosynthesize in low-light conditions or in deep waters. Other algae can store excess nutrients as starch or oil, which can be used during periods of nutrient limitation or stress. Additionally, some algae can form symbiotic relationships with other organisms, such as corals or fungi, and provide them with nutrients and energy.

Discussion of the Role of Algae in Various Ecosystems

Algae play critical roles in various aquatic ecosystems, serving as primary producers, forming the base of the food chain, and cycling nutrients and carbon. In freshwater environments, algae are essential for maintaining water quality and supporting fish and other aquatic organisms. They can also form harmful algal blooms (HABs) that produce toxins that can harm human health, wildlife, and the environment.

In marine environments, algae are the primary producers that support the ocean food chain. They are also critical for the global carbon cycle, as they fix carbon through photosynthesis and sequester it in the deep ocean. Algae also produce oxygen through photosynthesis, and it is estimated that they are responsible for about 50% of the world's oxygen production.

The Importance of Algae in the Global Carbon Cycle and Oxygen Production

Algae are major players in the global carbon cycle, accounting for about 45% of the ocean's primary production and fixing an estimated 50 billion tons of carbon per year. When algae die, they sink to the bottom of the ocean, taking carbon with them and sequestering it in the deep ocean. This process, called the biological pump, is one of the major ways that carbon is removed from the atmosphere and stored in the ocean.

In addition to their role in the carbon cycle, algae are also important producers of oxygen. Through photosynthesis, they produce an estimated 50% of the world's oxygen. This oxygen is essential for supporting terrestrial and aquatic life, as well as for maintaining the Earth's atmospheric composition.

Understanding the physiology of algae is crucial for comprehending their ecological roles and adaptations. In this chapter, we explore the fundamental aspects of algal physiology, including their photosynthetic mechanisms, nutrient uptake, and growth strategies.

SECTION 1: THE FUNDAMENTAL ASPECTS OF ALGAL PHYSIOLOGY

1.1 PHOTOSYNTHESIS IN ALGAE

Photosynthesis is a key physiological process in algae, enabling them to convert sunlight into chemical energy. Algae possess chloroplasts that contain pigments such as chlorophylls, carotenoids, and phycobilins, which absorb light energy. Through photosynthesis, algae fix carbon dioxide (CO_2) and produce oxygen (O_2) as byproducts. This process plays a vital role in the global carbon cycle and the production of atmospheric oxygen.

1.2 NUTRIENT UPTAKE AND ASSIMILATION

Algae exhibit diverse strategies for nutrient uptake and assimilation. They can obtain essential nutrients such as nitrogen, phosphorus, and trace elements from their surrounding environments. Some algae are capable of fixing atmospheric nitrogen, while others rely on uptake from water or through symbiotic associations. Algae also vary in their ability to store and utilize nutrients, adapting to nutrient availability in their respective habitats.

1.3 GROWTH AND REPRODUCTION

Algae exhibit a wide range of growth strategies, which depend on factors such as light, temperature, nutrient availability, and competition. They can reproduce both asexually and sexually, with different mechanisms such as cell division, fragmentation, spore formation, and gamete production. These reproductive strategies contribute to the rapid growth and colonization abilities of algae in various ecosystems.

SECTION 2: ALGAE IN ECOSYSTEMS

2.1 ALGAE IN FRESHWATER ENVIRONMENTS

Algae are a diverse group of aquatic organisms that play critical roles in the functioning of ecosystems worldwide. Their physiological and ecological characteristics are shaped by their evolutionary history and environmental conditions, such as temperature, light, nutrient availability, and water chemistry. In this chapter, we will provide an overview of the physiology and ecology of algae, discuss the role of algae in various ecosystems, and highlight the importance of algae in the global carbon cycle and oxygen production.

Algae have unique physiological adaptations that allow them to survive and thrive in a wide range of environmental conditions. For example, some algae can change their pigment composition and adjust their photosynthetic machinery to different light spectra, allowing them to photosynthesize in low-light conditions or in deep waters. Other algae can store excess nutrients as starch or oil, which can be used during periods of nutrient limitation or stress. Additionally, some algae can form symbiotic relationships with other organisms, such as corals or fungi, and provide them with nutrients and energy (Graham et al., 2009; Huisman, 2018; Larkum et al., 2012; Raven, 2013).

Discussion of the Role of Algae in Various Ecosystems

Algae play critical roles in various aquatic ecosystems, serving as primary producers, forming the base of the food chain, and cycling nutrients and carbon. In freshwater environments, algae are essential for maintaining water quality and supporting fish and other aquatic organisms. They can also form harmful algal blooms (HABs) that produce toxins that can harm human health, wildlife, and the environment (Huisman, 2018; Stewart & Fitzgerald, 1980).

2.2 ALGAE IN MARINE ENVIRONMENTS

In marine environments, algae are the primary producers that support the ocean food chain. They are also critical for the global carbon cycle, as they fix carbon through photosynthesis and sequester it in the deep ocean. Algae also produce oxygen through photosynthesis, and it is estimated that they are responsible for about 50% of the world's oxygen production (Graham et al., 2009; Larkum et al., 2012; Raven, 2013; Round et al., 2014).

The Importance of Algae in the Global Carbon Cycle and Oxygen Production

Algae are major players in the global carbon cycle, accounting for about 45% of the ocean's primary production and fixing an estimated 50 billion tons of carbon per year. When algae die, they sink to the bottom of the ocean, taking carbon with them and sequestering it in the deep ocean. This process, called the biological pump, is one of the major ways that carbon is removed from the atmosphere and stored in the ocean (Graham et al., 2009; Larkum et al., 2012; Raven, 2013; Round et al., 2014).

SECTION 3: ALGAE AND THE GLOBAL CARBON CYCLE

In addition to their role in the carbon cycle, algae are also important producers of oxygen. Through photosynthesis, they produce an estimated 50% of the world's oxygen. This oxygen is essential for supporting terrestrial and aquatic life, as well as for maintaining the Earth's atmospheric composition (Graham et al., 2009; Larkum et al., 2012; Raven, 2013; Round et al., 2014). Through photosynthesis, algae remove carbon dioxide from the atmosphere, converting it into organic carbon. This process helps regulate atmospheric CO_2 levels and mitigates climate change by sequestering carbon in biomass and sediments. Algae are also involved in the production of dissolved organic carbon, which has implications for nutrient cycling and the overall functioning of aquatic ecosystems.

Furthermore, algae contribute significantly to oxygen production on Earth. Through photosynthesis, they release oxygen as a byproduct, accounting for a substantial portion of atmospheric oxygen. This oxygen production supports the respiration and survival of diverse organisms, from aquatic organisms to terrestrial life.

By studying the physiology and ecology of algae, we gain a profound appreciation for their vital roles in sustaining ecosystems, regulating carbon dioxide levels, and supporting oxygen production. In the subsequent chapters, we will further explore the intricate interactions of algae with their environments, their responses to environmental changes, and their applications in various fields.

Embark on this enlightening journey as we delve deeper into the fascinating world of algae physiology and ecology. Through understanding their photosynthetic mechanisms, nutrient uptake, growth strategies, and reproductive processes, we gain insights into the remarkable adaptations that allow algae to thrive in diverse environments.

In freshwater ecosystems, algae serve as the primary producers, driving the food web and providing nourishment for a wide range of aquatic organisms. However, the excessive growth of algae, particularly during algal blooms, can have detrimental effects, leading to oxygen depletion and ecological disruptions. We will explore the factors that contribute to the formation of algal blooms and their ecological consequences.

In marine environments, algae play a crucial role in sustaining the productivity and biodiversity of coastal areas and open ocean regions. They contribute significantly to primary production and nutrient cycling, supporting intricate food webs and providing habitats for marine organisms. The formation of coral reefs, coastal protection by seaweeds and kelp forests, and their role as carbon sinks highlight the ecological importance of algae in marine ecosystems.

The significance of algae extends beyond individual ecosystems, as they play a central role in the global carbon cycle. By sequestering carbon dioxide through photosynthesis, algae help regulate atmospheric CO_2 levels, mitigating the impacts of climate change. Additionally, their oxygen production is essential for maintaining the balance of atmospheric gases, supporting life on Earth.

As we explore the physiology and ecology of algae, we gain a deeper appreciation for their multifaceted contributions to the functioning of ecosystems and their broader significance in global biogeochemical processes. The subsequent chapters will build upon this foundation, delving into specific aspects of algal physiology, ecological interactions, and their applications in fields such as biotechnology, environmental monitoring, and biofuel production.

Join us on this enlightening exploration as we unravel the intricate mechanisms and ecological roles of algae, deepening our understanding of these remarkable organisms and their impact on the planet we call home.

Conclusion

Algae are a diverse and important group of aquatic organisms that play critical roles in the functioning of ecosystems worldwide. Their physiology and ecology are shaped by their evolutionary history and environmental conditions, and they have unique adaptations that allow them to survive and thrive in a wide range of habitats. Algae are essential for maintaining water quality, supporting the ocean food chain, cycling nutrients and carbon, and producing oxygen. Understanding the physiology and ecology of algae is critical for managing

CHAPTER 4

Algae and Human Health

Algae are a diverse group of aquatic organisms that have been used by humans for various purposes, including medicine and food production. In recent years, there has been growing interest in the potential health benefits of algae consumption. However, there are also risks associated with algae consumption, including the occurrence of harmful algal blooms (HABs). In this chapter, we will explore the use of algae in medicine and food production, the potential health benefits of algae consumption, and the risks associated with algae consumption, including HABs.

The Use of Algae in Medicine and Food Production

Algae have been used in traditional medicine for centuries, and modern research has confirmed their potential therapeutic benefits. For example, certain types of algae contain compounds that have anti-inflammatory, antiviral, and anticancer properties. Some algae also contain high levels of antioxidants, which can help protect cells from oxidative damage (Graham et al., 2009; Huisman, 2018; Larkum et al., 2012; Raven, 2013).

Algae are also used in food production, particularly in the production of food supplements and additives. For example, spirulina, a type of blue-green algae, is a popular food supplement due to its high protein content and antioxidant properties. Other types of algae, such as seaweed, are used as ingredients in various foods, including sushi, soups, and salads (Graham et al., 2009; Huisman, 2018; Larkum et al., 2012; Raven, 2013; Round et al., 2014).

Potential Health Benefits of Algae Consumption

There is growing evidence to suggest that algae consumption may have several health benefits. For example, studies have shown that consuming spirulina can help reduce inflammation and improve blood lipid levels in people with diabetes. Other studies have suggested that consuming seaweed may help reduce the risk of heart disease, due to its high levels of fiber and antioxidants (Graham et al., 2009; Larkum et al., 2012; Raven, 2013)

Algae are also rich in various vitamins and minerals, including vitamin B12, iron, and calcium. For people who follow a plant-based diet, algae can be an important source of these essential nutrients (Graham et al., 2009; Larkum et al., 2012; Raven, 2013).

Risks Associated with Algae Consumption, Including Harmful Algal Blooms

Despite the potential health benefits of algae consumption, there are also risks associated with consuming algae, particularly in the form of supplements or in areas where HABs occur. HABs are the result of the rapid growth of certain types of algae, which can produce toxins that can be harmful to humans and animals.

Symptoms of algae poisoning can include gastrointestinal problems, skin irritation, and respiratory problems. In severe cases, algae poisoning can lead to liver damage and even death. To reduce the risk of algae poisoning, it is important to avoid consuming algae from areas where HABs are known to occur and to follow guidelines for safe algae consumption (Graham et al., 2009; Huisman, 2018; Larkum et al., 2012; Raven, 2013; Round et al., 2014; Stewart & Fitzgerald, 1980).

SECTION 1: ALGAE IN MEDICINE

Algae have been used in traditional medicine systems for centuries and continue to play a significant role in modern medicine. In this chapter, we explore the diverse applications of algae in medicine and the potential health benefits they offer.

1.1 MEDICINAL PROPERTIES OF ALGAE

Certain species of algae contain bioactive compounds that possess therapeutic properties. These compounds include polysaccharides, polyphenols, pigments, and fatty acids, which have been studied for their antioxidant, anti-inflammatory, antimicrobial, and anticancer effects. We delve into the specific algae species that have been investigated for their medicinal properties and the ongoing research in this field.

1.2 ALGAE-DERIVED PHARMACEUTICALS

Algae serve as a valuable source of pharmaceutical compounds. They have been utilized in the production of drugs and therapeutics, including antibiotics, antivirals, antifungals, anti-inflammatory agents, and anticancer drugs. We explore the advancements in algal biotechnology that have facilitated the extraction and production of these valuable compounds for medical purposes.

SECTION 2: ALGAE IN FOOD PRODUCTION

Algae have long been utilized as a source of food and nutritional supplements. In this section, we examine the use of algae in food production and its potential as a sustainable and nutrient-rich food source.

2.1 CULINARY USES OF ALGAE

Certain types of algae, such as seaweed and microalgae, are consumed as food in various cultures around the world. We explore the culinary traditions and techniques associated with algae consumption, highlighting the nutritional value and unique flavours they offer. From sushi rolls wrapped in nori to spirulina-infused smoothies, algae have found their way into diverse culinary creations.

2.2 ALGAE AS NUTRITIONAL SUPPLEMENTS

Algae-based nutritional supplements have gained popularity due to their high nutrient content. They are rich in vitamins, minerals, essential fatty acids, protein, and antioxidants. We delve into the potential health benefits of consuming algae-based supplements, such as boosting immunity, supporting cardiovascular health, promoting brain function, and enhancing overall well-being.

SECTION 3: RISKS ASSOCIATED WITH ALGAE CONSUMPTION

While algae offer numerous health benefits, it is important to acknowledge and understand the potential risks associated with their consumption. We address the issue of harmful algal blooms (HABs), which occur when certain species of algae produce toxins that can contaminate water bodies and pose risks to human and animal health. We discuss the causes of HABs, their impact on ecosystems and public health, and the measures taken to monitor and manage these occurrences.

By exploring the diverse applications of algae in medicine and food production, we gain insights into the potential benefits they offer for human health and well-being. However, we also recognize the importance of understanding and mitigating the risks associated with algae consumption, particularly in the context of harmful algal blooms. This chapter aims to provide a comprehensive overview of the complex relationship between algae and human health, highlighting both the promising opportunities and the need for caution.

SECTION 4: ALGAE AND BIOTECHNOLOGY

Algae possess remarkable properties that have made them a valuable resource in various biotechnological applications. In this section, we delve into the potential of algae in biotechnology and their contributions to fields such as biofuel production, wastewater treatment, and environmental monitoring.

4.1 ALGAE AS A SOURCE OF BIOFUELS

Algae have gained attention as a promising source of renewable biofuels. Certain species of microalgae can produce high amounts of lipids, which can be converted into biofuels such as biodiesel. We explore the cultivation methods, lipid extraction techniques, and the challenges involved in scaling up algae-based biofuel production. The use of algae in biofuels not only offers a potential alternative to fossil fuels but also mitigates greenhouse gas emissions.

4.2 ALGAE IN WASTEWATER TREATMENT

Algae demonstrate a remarkable ability to absorb nutrients, including nitrogen and phosphorus, from wastewater. This property has led to their use in wastewater treatment systems, where they help remove pollutants and restore water quality. We examine the role of algae in wastewater treatment, their interactions with other treatment processes, and the potential for sustainable and cost-effective wastewater management.

4.3 ALGAE IN ENVIRONMENTAL MONITORING

Algae serve as valuable indicators of environmental health and water quality. Their response to changes in nutrient levels, temperature, and pollution can provide insights into ecosystem dynamics. We discuss the use of algae in environmental monitoring programs, including the assessment of water pollution, ecosystem health, and the impacts of climate change. Algal monitoring plays a crucial role in managing and preserving the integrity of aquatic ecosystems.

SECTION 5: FUTURE DIRECTIONS AND CHALLENGES

The exploration of algae in medicine, food production, and biotechnology holds significant promise. However, several challenges must be addressed for the realization of their full potential. These challenges include optimizing cultivation methods, improving extraction and processing techniques, ensuring sustainable production practices, and addressing regulatory considerations. We discuss these challenges and highlight the ongoing research and innovations aimed at overcoming them.

In this chapter, we have explored the diverse applications of algae in human health, their potential as a sustainable food source, and their role in biotechnological advancements. From their medicinal properties to their contributions to biofuel production and environmental monitoring, algae continue to shape various aspects of human life. Understanding their potential benefits and the associated risks allows us to harness their power responsibly and explore innovative solutions for a healthier and more sustainable future.

CHAPTER 5

Algae Biotechnology

Algae have gained attention in recent years as a potential source of renewable energy and as a means of reducing carbon emissions. In addition to their potential use in biofuel production and carbon capture, algae also have other applications in biotechnology, including wastewater treatment and the production of bioplastics (Huisman, 2018; Raven, 2013; Round, Chapman, & Maberly, 2014; Van der Meer, 2015).

The Use of Algae in Biofuel Production and Carbon Capture

Algae are a promising source of renewable energy, as they can be used to produce biofuels such as biodiesel, bioethanol, and biogas (Raven, 2013; Round et al., 2014). Algae can grow rapidly and have high lipid and carbohydrate content, which makes them an attractive source of biomass for fuel production. Additionally, algae can be grown using wastewater or other low-quality water sources, reducing the demand for freshwater resources (Huisman, 2018; Round et al., 2014).

Algae can also be used in carbon capture and sequestration. As algae grow, they absorb carbon dioxide from the atmosphere, reducing greenhouse gas emissions. The algae can then be harvested and processed to produce biofuels or other products, effectively capturing and storing carbon (Huisman, 2018; Round et al., 2014).

The Salton Sea is a large, shallow, saline lake located in California's Imperial Valley. Due to agricultural runoff and other sources of pollution, the Salton Sea has experienced ecological problems, including harmful algal blooms, fish die-offs, and reduced oxygen levels in the water (Stewart & Fitzgerald, 1980).

Algae play a significant role in the ecology of the Salton Sea, as they are the primary source of food for the fish and other aquatic organisms that live there. However, the excessive growth of algae, particularly cyanobacteria, can lead to harmful algal blooms, which can produce toxins that are harmful to fish, wildlife, and humans (Stewart & Fitzgerald, 1980).

Efforts are underway to address the ecological problems at the Salton Sea, including the development of programs to reduce nutrient runoff from agricultural sources and the restoration of wetlands and other habitats that support a diverse range of aquatic species (Stewart & Fitzgerald, 1980).

In India, algae have been used in various applications for centuries, particularly in traditional medicine and food production (Watanabe & Hattori, 2001). For example, spirulina, a type of blue-green algae, is cultivated in parts of India for use as a nutritional supplement and in the production of various food products (Watanabe & Hattori, 2001).

Algae are also being explored as a potential source of renewable energy in India. Several research projects and pilot programs have been launched to explore the use of algae in biofuel production, particularly in areas where land is limited and traditional sources of biofuel, such as sugarcane, are not practical (Watanabe & Hattori, 2001).

Overall, algae play an important role in both the ecology and the economy of the Salton Sea area and in India. As research continues to explore the potential uses of algae in various applications, we may discover new and innovative ways to harness the power of these versatile organisms (Huisman, 2018; Watanabe & Hattori, 2001).

Other Potential Applications of Algae in Biotechnology

In addition to their potential use in biofuel production and carbon capture, algae have other potential applications in biotechnology. For example, algae can be used in wastewater treatment, where they can absorb nutrients and other contaminants from the water, effectively purifying it. This approach, known as phytoremediation, can be an effective and environmentally friendly way to treat wastewater (Huisman, 2018; Raven, 2013).

Algae can also be used in the production of bioplastics, which are plastics made from renewable sources such as plant material. Some types of algae contain polysaccharides, which can be used to produce biodegradable plastics that are both renewable and environmentally friendly (Huisman, 2018; Raven, 2013).

SECTION 1: ALGAE IN BIOFUEL PRODUCTION

Algae have emerged as a promising source of renewable energy, particularly in the production of biofuels. In this chapter, we explore the utilization of algae in biofuel production and their potential as a sustainable alternative to fossil fuels (Huisman, 2018; Raven, 2013; Round et al., 2014).

1.1 ALGAE-BASED BIOFUELS

Certain species of microalgae have the ability to accumulate high levels of lipids, which can be converted into biofuels such as biodiesel. We delve into the cultivation techniques, lipid extraction methods, and refining processes involved in algae-based biofuel production. The advantages of algae as a biofuel feedstock, including their high growth rates, ability to thrive in various environments, and minimal competition for arable land, make them a promising option in the quest for renewable energy sources (Huisman, 2018; Raven, 2013; Round et al., 2014).

1.2 CARBON CAPTURE AND ALGAE

Algae play a significant role in carbon capture and storage. Through photosynthesis, they absorb carbon dioxide (CO_2) from the atmosphere and convert it into organic biomass. We explore the potential of algae in mitigating greenhouse gas emissions and their use in carbon capture technologies. By harnessing the growth and carbon-fixing capabilities of algae, we can reduce CO2 levels and contribute to the fight against climate change (Huisman, 2018; Raven, 2013; Round et al., 2014).

SECTION 2: OTHER APPLICATIONS OF ALGAE IN BIOTECHNOLOGY

2.1 ALGAE IN WASTEWATER TREATMENT

Algae exhibit an exceptional ability to remove nutrients, such as nitrogen and phosphorus, from wastewater. This property has led to their use in wastewater treatment systems, where they help purify and remediate polluted water. We discuss the application of algae in wastewater treatment, their role in nutrient removal and oxygenation, and the potential for sustainable and eco-friendly wastewater management practices (Huisman, 2018; Raven, 2013).

2.2 ALGAE IN BIOPLASTICS PRODUCTION

The production of bioplastics from renewable sources is gaining attention as an alternative to petroleum-based plastics. Algae offer a potential solution as a sustainable feedstock for bioplastics production. We explore the use of algae in the synthesis of biodegradable plastics, their advantages over traditional plastics, and the challenges associated with large-scale production and commercialization (Huisman, 2018; Raven, 2013).

2.3 ALGAE-DERIVED NUTRACEUTICALS AND COSMETICS

Algae are rich in bioactive compounds, including antioxidants, pigments, polysaccharides, and omega-3 fatty acids. These compounds have potential applications in the nutraceutical and cosmetic industries. We delve into the extraction and utilization of algae-derived compounds for the development of functional foods, dietary supplements, skincare products, and cosmetics. The unique properties of algae make them an intriguing source of natural ingredients with potential health and beauty benefits (Huisman, 2018; Raven, 2013).

SECTION 3: FUTURE PROSPECTS AND CHALLENGES

While algae biotechnology shows great promise in various fields, there are still challenges to overcome for its widespread implementation. These challenges include optimizing cultivation techniques, improving productivity and efficiency, developing cost-effective extraction and processing methods, and ensuring sustainable and environmentally friendly practices. We discuss these challenges and highlight the ongoing research and innovations aimed at addressing them (Huisman, 2018; Raven, 2013; Round et al., 2014).

In this chapter, we have explored the diverse applications of algae in biotechnology, ranging from biofuel production and carbon capture to wastewater treatment and bioplastics synthesis. The potential of algae as a renewable resource and their ability to address environmental and sustainability concerns make them a subject of significant interest and ongoing research (Huisman, 2018; Raven, 2013; Round et al., 2014).

SECTION 4: ALGAE IN AGRICULTURE AND AQUACULTURE

Algae have valuable applications in the agricultural and aquaculture sectors, offering sustainable solutions for nutrient management, animal feed, and soil health. In this section, we explore the potential of algae in improving agricultural practices and enhancing aquaculture production (Burrows, 1991; Graham et al., 2009; Guiry & Guiry, 2021).

4.1 ALGAE AS FERTILIZERS AND SOIL AMENDMENTS

Certain species of algae, such as seaweeds, are rich in essential nutrients, including nitrogen, phosphorus, and potassium, as well as trace elements. We discuss the use of algae as organic fertilizers and soil amendments, and their role in enhancing nutrient availability, soil structure, and microbial activity. Algae-based fertilizers provide a sustainable alternative to chemical fertilizers, promoting environmentally friendly and nutrient-efficient agricultural practices (Burrows, 1991; Graham et al., 2009; Guiry & Guiry, 2021).

4.2 ALGAE IN ANIMAL FEED

Algae offer a nutritious and sustainable alternative for animal feed, particularly in aquaculture and livestock industries. Microalgae, such as spirulina and chlorella, are rich in proteins, essential amino acids, vitamins, and minerals. We explore the incorporation of algae into animal diets, their impact on growth, health, and product quality, and the potential for reducing the dependence on traditional feed sources, such as fishmeal (Burrows, 1991; Graham et al., 2009; Guiry & Guiry, 2021).

SECTION 5: INNOVATIONS AND FUTURE DIRECTIONS

The field of algae biotechnology is continuously evolving, with ongoing research and innovations driving new applications and advancements. In this section, we discuss emerging trends and future prospects in algae biotechnology (Huisman, 2018; Raven, 2013; Van der Meer, 2015).

5.1 GENETIC ENGINEERING AND ALGAE BIOTECHNOLOGY

Advances in genetic engineering and synthetic biology have opened up new possibilities for manipulating algae to enhance desired traits and optimize their biotechnological potential. We explore the use of genetic engineering techniques to improve algae productivity, lipid content, and the production of valuable compounds. Genetic engineering holds promise for tailoring algae strains for specific applications, further expanding their potential in biotechnology (Huisman, 2018; Raven, 2013; Van der Meer, 2015).

5.2 ALGAE CULTIVATION SYSTEMS AND SCALING UP

Efficient and scalable cultivation systems are crucial for the successful implementation of algae biotechnology. We discuss various cultivation methods, including open ponds, photobioreactors, and closed systems, their advantages, limitations, and the challenges associated with scaling up algae production. The development of innovative cultivation technologies and optimization of cultivation parameters are key areas of focus to meet the growing demand for algae-based products (Huisman, 2018; Raven, 2013; Van der Meer, 2015).

SECTION 6: CONCLUSION

In this chapter, we have explored the diverse applications of algae in biotechnology, ranging from biofuel production and carbon capture to wastewater treatment, bioplastics, agriculture, and aquaculture. The unique properties of algae, including their rapid growth, high productivity, and ability to thrive in diverse environments, make them a valuable resource for sustainable solutions in various industries.

The continuous advancements in algae biotechnology offer promising opportunities for addressing global challenges such as climate change, resource scarcity, and environmental pollution. By harnessing the potential of algae and combining it with innovative technologies, we can pave the way for a more sustainable and eco-friendly future.

CHAPTER 6

Algae Conservation and Future Directions

Algae play a crucial role in ecosystems around the world, providing food and habitat for a wide variety of aquatic organisms (Graham et al., 2009; Round et al., 2014). However, like many other organisms, algae populations are facing a range of threats, including pollution, climate change, and habitat destruction. In this chapter, we will discuss the threats facing algae populations and the importance of conservation efforts. We will also provide an overview of current research on algae and future directions in the field of algology (Graham et al., 2009; Round et al., 2014).

Threats Facing Algae Populations and the Importance of Conservation Efforts

Algae populations are facing a range of threats, including pollution, climate change, and habitat destruction. Pollution from agricultural runoff, wastewater discharge, and other sources can lead to excessive nutrient levels in water bodies, promoting the growth of harmful algal blooms (Round et al., 2014; Stewart & Fitzgerald, 1980). Climate change, including warming waters and changes in precipitation patterns, can also affect algae populations, as well as the organisms that rely on them for food and habitat (Graham et al., 2009; Round et al., 2014). Habitat destruction, such as the destruction of wetlands and other important algae habitats, can also have a significant impact on algae populations (Round et al., 2014).

Conservation efforts are critical for protecting algae populations and the ecosystems they support. These efforts may include the protection and restoration of wetlands, the reduction of nutrient runoff and other sources of pollution, and the development of sustainable practices for the use of algae in various applications (Stewart & Fitzgerald, 1980; Round et al., 2014).

Overview of Current Research on Algae and Future Directions in the Field of Algology

Research on algae is ongoing, with scientists exploring new and innovative ways to harness the power of these versatile organisms. Current research in the field of algology includes the development of new methods for algae cultivation, the exploration of algae's potential as a source of renewable energy, and the investigation of algae's role in biogeochemical cycles and carbon sequestration (Huisman, 2018; Raven, 2013; Van der Meer, 2015).

Future directions in the field of algology may include the development of new technologies for algae cultivation and harvesting, the identification of new species of algae with unique properties, and the exploration of algae's potential in fields such as medicine and biotechnology (Huisman, 2018; Raven, 2013; Van der Meer, 2015). Additionally, there may be a greater focus on understanding the complex interactions between algae and other organisms in aquatic ecosystems and the potential impacts of environmental stressors on these interactions (Round et al., 2014).

SECTION 1: THREATS TO ALGAE POPULATIONS

Algae, despite their abundance and ecological significance, face numerous threats that impact their populations and habitats. In this chapter, we delve into the challenges and conservation efforts aimed at preserving algae diversity and ecosystems.

1.1 POLLUTION AND HABITAT DEGRADATION

Pollution from industrial and agricultural activities poses a significant threat to algae populations. Runoff containing excess nutrients, such as nitrogen and phosphorus, can lead to harmful algal blooms and disrupt ecosystem balance. We discuss the impact of pollution on algae habitats, including freshwater and marine environments, and the importance of mitigating pollution to safeguard their populations (Graham et al., 2009; Round et al., 2014).

1.2 CLIMATE CHANGE AND OCEAN ACIDIFICATION

Climate change and ocean acidification pose substantial challenges to algae populations. Rising temperatures, changes in rainfall patterns, and increased carbon dioxide levels affect the growth and distribution of algae species. We explore the implications of climate change and ocean acidification on algae ecosystems and their potential cascading effects on marine food webs and biodiversity (Graham et al., 2009; Round et al., 2014).

SECTION 2 ALGAE CONSERVATION EFFORTS

2.1 PROTECTED AREAS AND CONSERVATION INITIATIVES

Conserving important habitats and establishing protected areas are essential strategies for preserving algae populations. We discuss the significance of marine protected areas, coastal management practices, and the integration of algae conservation within broader ecosystem conservation efforts. Highlighting successful conservation initiatives, we emphasize the need for collaborative approaches involving scientists, policymakers, and local communities (Graham et al., 2009; Round et al., 2014).

2.2 RESTORATION AND REHABILITATION PROGRAMS

In cases where algae habitats have been degraded, restoration and rehabilitation programs play a crucial role in recovering and enhancing their populations. We explore the methods used in restoring algae habitats, including the reintroduction of native species, habitat modification, and the promotion of sustainable practices to reduce pollution and habitat degradation (Graham et al., 2009; Round et al., 2014).

SECTION 3 CURRENT RESEARCH AND FUTURE DIRECTIONS

3.1 ADVANCEMENTS IN ALGOLOGICAL RESEARCH

Algological research continues to expand our understanding of algae and their ecological significance. We provide an overview of current research topics, including the exploration of algal biodiversity, molecular and genomic studies, and the development of novel applications in fields such as biotechnology and environmental monitoring. The integration of interdisciplinary approaches and the use of advanced technologies drive the future directions of algological research (Graham et al., 2009; Round et al., 2014).

3.2 ALGAE IN BIOREMEDIATION AND CLIMATE MITIGATION

The potential of algae in bioremediation and climate mitigation holds promise for addressing environmental challenges. We discuss ongoing research on the use of algae for wastewater treatment, carbon sequestration, and nutrient recycling. The application of algae in these areas not only offers ecological benefits but also contributes to sustainable development and the restoration of degraded ecosystems (Graham et al., 2009; Round et al., 2014).

SECTION 4 CONCLUSION AND CONTINUING

In this chapter, we have explored the threats facing algae populations and the importance of conservation efforts in preserving their diversity and ecosystems. Pollution, climate change, and habitat degradation pose significant challenges, emphasizing the urgency of proactive conservation measures.

Furthermore, we have discussed the current research trends in algology and the future directions that will drive the field forward. From molecular studies to applications in biotechnology and environmental management, algological research presents exciting opportunities for understanding and harnessing the potential of algae.

As we conclude this chapter, we encourage continued efforts in algae conservation, the integration of algae research into environmental decision-making processes, and the exploration of sustainable practices to mitigate the threats facing algae populations. By safeguarding the diversity and health of algae, we ensure the ecological integrity of our ecosystems and pave the way for a more sustainable and biodiverse future.

SECTION 5 ALGAE EDUCATION AND PUBLIC AWARENESS

5.1 IMPORTANCE OF ALGAE EDUCATION

Effective education and public awareness play a vital role in promoting algae conservation and fostering a deeper understanding of their ecological significance. We discuss the importance of incorporating algology into science curricula at various educational levels, as well as the need for public outreach programs and initiatives to raise awareness about the value of algae and the threats they face. By enhancing algological knowledge among students and the general public, we can cultivate a sense of stewardship and inspire action for algae conservation (Graham et al., 2009; Round et al., 2014).

5.2 CITIZEN SCIENCE AND ALGAE MONITORING

Engaging the public in algae monitoring through citizen science initiatives can provide valuable data on algae distribution, abundance, and ecological changes. We explore the role of citizen science in algae research and conservation, highlighting the opportunities for individuals to contribute to scientific knowledge and promote community involvement in protecting algae populations. Citizen science programs can foster a sense of ownership and empowerment, making people active participants in the conservation of algae and their ecosystems (Graham et al., 2009; Round et al., 2014).

                                              ALL ABOUT ALGAE

SECTION 6: FUTURE DIRECTIONS IN ALGOLOGY

6.1 SUSTAINABLE ALGAE CULTIVATION

The development of sustainable algae cultivation methods is crucial for meeting the increasing demand for algae-based products while minimizing environmental impacts. We discuss the importance of optimizing cultivation techniques, improving resource efficiency, and exploring innovative approaches such as integrated multitrophic aquaculture and land-based cultivation systems. Sustainable algae cultivation practices ensure the long-term viability of algae resources and their contributions to various sectors (Graham et al., 2009; Round et al., 2014).

6.2 EMERGING APPLICATIONS AND INNOVATIONS

The field of algology continues to evolve, presenting new opportunities for innovation and application. We explore emerging areas of research, such as the use of algae in biofabrication, pharmaceuticals, and bioremediation. Additionally, we discuss the potential of algae in sustainable food production, including algae-based protein sources and the development of novel culinary applications. These advancements hold promise for addressing global challenges and advancing the role of algae in sustainable development (Graham et al., 2009; Round et al., 2014).

SECTION 7 CONCLUSION

In this chapter, we have highlighted the importance of algae education, public awareness, and citizen science in promoting algae conservation. By empowering individuals and communities with knowledge and engagement, we can work collectively to protect and conserve algae populations and their ecosystems.

We have also explored future directions in algology, emphasizing the need for sustainable cultivation practices and the potential of algae in emerging fields. As research and innovation continue to unfold, the possibilities for algae in addressing environmental, nutritional, and industrial challenges are expanding.

By recognizing the significance of algae, their vulnerabilities, and their potential, we can ensure the conservation of these vital organisms and harness their benefits in a sustainable and responsible manner. Let us forge ahead in exploring and safeguarding the remarkable world of algae for the well-being of our planet and future generations.

CHAPTER 7

Algae in Art and Design

Algae are not just important for their ecological and economic value; they have also become a source of inspiration for artists and designers around the world. In this chapter, we will explore the use of algae in art, fashion, and product design, as well as highlight examples of artists and designers who incorporate algae into their work.

The Use of Algae in Art, Fashion, and Product Design

Algae's unique properties, such as their vibrant colours and textures, have inspired artists and designers to incorporate them into their work. Algae have been used in a variety of artistic mediums, including painting, sculpture, and photography. In fashion, designers have used algae-based materials to create sustainable and eco-friendly clothing, while in product design, algae-based materials have been used to create biodegradable packaging and other products.

Examples of Artists and Designers Who Incorporate Algae into Their Work

Many artists and designers have explored the use of algae in their work, creating pieces that showcase the beauty and versatility of these organisms. Here are a few examples:

- Lia Giraud: Lia Giraud is a French artist who works with algae and other materials to create sculptures and installations that explore the relationships between humans and the natural world. Her work often incorporates living algae, which grow and change over time (Graham et al., 2009; Round et al., 2014).

- Suzanne Lee: Suzanne Lee is a fashion designer who has worked with algae-based materials to create sustainable and eco-friendly clothing. Her work has been featured in museums and galleries around the world (Graham et al., 2009; Round et al., 2014).

- Studio Klarenbeek & Dros: Studio Klarenbeek & Dros is a design studio that creates products using algae-based materials. Their products include biodegradable packaging and other products that are designed to be sustainable and environmentally friendly (Graham et al., 2009; Round et al., 2014).

- Sarah Roberts: Sarah Roberts is a British artist who creates paintings and prints inspired by the patterns and textures of algae. Her work is characterized by its vibrant colours and intricate details (Graham et al., 2009; Round et al., 2014).

SECTION 1: ALGAE AS A SOURCE OF INSPIRATION

Algae, with its mesmerizing shapes, vibrant colours, and unique biological properties, have long been a source of inspiration for artists and designers. In this chapter, we explore the fascinating intersection of algae with art, fashion, and product design, showcasing the creative ways in which algae find expression in these fields.

1.1 ALGAE AS A MEDIUM OF ARTISTIC EXPRESSION

Algae offer artists a captivating medium for artistic expression. We delve into the use of algae in various art forms, including painting, sculpture, and installation art. From capturing the intricate forms and patterns of algae to exploring their symbolism and ecological themes, artists have been inspired by the beauty and significance of algae in their creative endeavours (Graham et al., 2009; Round et al., 2014).

1.2 ALGAE IN FASHION AND TEXTILE DESIGN

Algae have also found their way into the world of fashion and textile design. We explore the incorporation of algae-based materials in clothing, accessories, and textile production. Algae-based fabrics, such as seaweed-derived fibres, offer sustainable alternatives to traditional textiles, showcasing the potential of algae in reducing the environmental impact of the fashion industry (Graham et al., 2009; Round et al., 2014).

SECTION 2: ALGAE-INSPIRED DESIGN AND PRODUCTS

2.1 BIOMIMICRY AND ALGAE-INSPIRED DESIGN

The biomimicry approach draws inspiration from nature, including algae, to design innovative and sustainable products. We explore examples of algae-inspired design, where the form, structure, and functions of algae are translated into practical applications. Algae-inspired designs often optimize efficiency, adaptability, and resource utilization, highlighting the ingenious solutions nature provides (Graham et al., 2009; Round et al., 2014).

2.2 ALGAE-BASED PRODUCTS

Algae are increasingly being utilized as a renewable resource for the production of various products. We discuss the development of algae-based materials, such as bioplastics, dyes, and pigments, which offer eco-friendly alternatives to conventional materials. Additionally, we explore the use of algae in the creation of skincare products, cosmetics, and even algae-based food products, showcasing the versatility and potential of algae in product development (Graham et al., 2009; Round et al., 2014).

SECTION 3 ARTISTS AND DESIGNERS INCORPORATING ALGAE

3.1 ALGAE-BASED ART AND DESIGN PRACTITIONERS

We profile artists and designers who actively incorporate algae into their work, pushing the boundaries of creativity and sustainability. From bioartists who use living algae in their installations to designers who explore algae as a material for product design, we showcase the visionaries who merge art, design, and algae to provoke thought, raise awareness, and reimagine our relationship with nature (Graham et al., 2009; Round et al., 2014).

We have explored the captivating realm of algae in art and design. From serving as a medium of artistic expression to inspiring sustainable fashion, textiles, and product design, algae offer a rich source of inspiration and materials for creative endeavours.

The integration of algae in art and design not only brings aesthetic beauty but also highlights the ecological significance of these organisms. By incorporating algae into various artistic and design practices, we deepen our connection with nature and raise awareness about the importance of environmental conservation.

4.1 ALGAE AS A SYMBOL OF ENVIRONMENTAL CONCERN

In addition to their aesthetic and functional qualities, algae also serve as a powerful symbol of environmental awareness. We explore how artists and designers use algae in their work to highlight pressing ecological issues, such as water pollution, climate change, and habitat degradation. Through their artistic expressions, they encourage dialogue and action, fostering a deeper understanding of the importance of algae and the urgent need to protect our natural environment (Graham et al., 2009; Round et al., 2014).

4.2 ALGAE-BASED INSTALLATIONS AND ACTIVISM

Art installations and activist projects centred around algae have gained prominence as means of raising awareness about environmental challenges. We showcase examples of large-scale installations and public artworks that incorporate algae as a central element, captivating audiences and provoking contemplation. These projects serve as a catalyst for discussions on sustainability, pollution, and the interconnectedness of ecosystems (Graham et al., 2009; Round et al., 2014).

SECTION 5: ALGAE IN INDIGENOUS ART AND CULTURAL HERITAGE

5.1 ALGAE IN INDIGENOUS ARTISTIC TRADITIONS

Indigenous cultures around the world have long recognized the significance of algae and incorporated them into their artistic traditions. We delve into the rich heritage of algae-inspired artwork in indigenous communities, highlighting the cultural symbolism, spiritual meanings, and sustainable practices associated with algae. By exploring these indigenous perspectives, we deepen our appreciation for the profound relationship between algae and human culture (Graham et al., 2009; Round et al., 2014).

5.2 TRADITIONAL KNOWLEDGE AND SUSTAINABLE PRACTICES

Indigenous communities possess valuable traditional knowledge about the sustainable use of algae and the preservation of their habitats. We examine how this knowledge is integrated into contemporary art and design, emphasizing the importance of cultural preservation and the transmission of ancestral wisdom. By celebrating indigenous artistic expressions, we honour the legacy of algae and foster respect for diverse cultural perspectives (Graham et al., 2009; Round et al., 2014).

SECTION 6 CONCLUSION

In this chapter, we have explored the multifaceted relationship between algae and art, fashion, and design. From inspiring creative expressions to symbolizing environmental concerns and celebrating indigenous cultural heritage, algae leave a lasting impact on artistic endeavours.

By incorporating algae into various forms of artistic expression, we engage audiences on a profound level, stirring emotions and deepening their understanding of ecological issues. Algae also serve as a reminder of the interconnectedness of all living beings and our responsibility to protect and preserve the natural world.

We encourage artists, designers, and enthusiasts to continue exploring the artistic possibilities of algae, to promote environmental awareness, and to draw inspiration from the beauty and significance of these remarkable organisms. By harnessing the creative potential of algae, we can contribute to a more sustainable and harmonious relationship between art, nature, and human society.

CHAPTER 8

Algae and Climate Change

Algae play a critical role in the Earth's carbon cycle, producing oxygen and absorbing carbon dioxide through photosynthesis. As such, they are essential to maintaining the planet's ecological balance. However, climate change is having a significant impact on algae populations and ecosystems, with potentially far-reaching consequences. In this chapter, we will explore the impact of climate change on algae populations and ecosystems, as well as the potential role of algae in mitigating climate change.

The Impact of Climate Change on Algae Populations and Ecosystems

Climate change is having a significant impact on the world's oceans, lakes, and rivers, affecting algae populations and ecosystems in a variety of ways. For example, rising temperatures can lead to an increase in harmful algal blooms, which can be toxic to humans and other animals. Changes in precipitation patterns and water availability can also affect algae populations, as can changes in ocean currents and salinity levels.

In addition to these direct impacts, climate change can also have indirect effects on algae populations and ecosystems. For example, changes in temperature and precipitation can affect the availability of nutrients and other resources that algae need to thrive. These changes can, in turn, affect the entire food chain, from small organisms like zooplankton to larger predators like fish and marine mammals (Graham et al., 2009; Round et al., 2014).

The Potential Role of Algae in Mitigating Climate Change

Despite the challenges that climate change poses for algae populations and ecosystems, algae may also have a role to play in mitigating climate change. For example, algae can be used to produce biofuels, which can replace fossil fuels and help reduce greenhouse gas emissions. Algae can also be used in carbon capture and storage systems, where they absorb carbon dioxide from the atmosphere and store it in their biomass (Graham et al., 2009; Round et al., 2014).

In addition to these applications, algae may also have other potential uses in mitigating climate change. For example, algae can be used in wastewater treatment systems to remove nutrients and pollutants from wastewater, reducing the environmental impact of human activities. Algae may also be used in agriculture, where they can help improve soil quality and reduce the use of synthetic fertilizers (Graham et al., 2009; Round et al., 2014).

SECTION 1: CLIMATE CHANGE AND ALGAE ECOSYSTEMS

Climate change poses significant challenges to algae populations and the ecosystems they inhabit. In this chapter, we delve into the impacts of climate change on algae and their ecological dynamics, highlighting the interconnectedness between algae and climate.

1.1 CHANGING ENVIRONMENTAL CONDITIONS

Algae are highly sensitive to changes in environmental conditions, and climate change brings about alterations in temperature, rainfall patterns, nutrient availability, and water chemistry. We discuss how these changes affect the distribution, abundance, and composition of algae populations, leading to shifts in ecosystems' structure and function. By understanding the specific responses of different algal groups to climate change, we can better comprehend the implications for ecosystem dynamics.

1.2 HARMFUL ALGAL BLOOMS AND CLIMATE CHANGE

The occurrence and severity of harmful algal blooms (HABs) are influenced by climate change. We explore the relationship between climate factors and HABs, discussing how warming temperatures, altered precipitation patterns, and nutrient runoff contribute to the proliferation of harmful algae. We also examine the ecological and socio-economic impacts of HABs on aquatic ecosystems, human health, and industries reliant on clean water resources.

SECTION 2: ALGAE AS CLIMATE CHANGE MITIGATORS

2.1 CARBON SEQUESTRATION AND ALGAL BLOOMS

Algae play a crucial role in the global carbon cycle and have the potential to mitigate climate change through carbon sequestration. We examine the ability of algae to capture and store atmospheric carbon dioxide through photosynthesis, both in marine and freshwater environments. We discuss the formation of algal blooms as a natural process that sequesters carbon and the potential for harnessing this phenomenon to enhance carbon capture and storage efforts.

2.2 ALGAE-BASED BIOFUELS AND RENEWABLE ENERGY

Algae have garnered attention as a promising source of renewable energy in the form of biofuels. We explore the potential of algae-based biofuel production as a means to reduce greenhouse gas emissions and mitigate climate change. We discuss the challenges and advancements in algae cultivation, harvesting, and conversion technologies, as well as the potential for algae-based biofuels to replace fossil fuels in various sectors.

SECTION 3: ALGAE AND CLIMATE CHANGE RESEARCH

3.1 STUDYING ALGAE RESPONSES TO CLIMATE CHANGE

Understanding how algae respond to climate change is vital for predicting future ecosystem dynamics and implementing effective mitigation strategies. We delve into ongoing research on the physiological, genetic, and ecological responses of algae to changing environmental conditions. By examining the adaptive mechanisms of algae and their resilience to climate change stressors, we gain insights into potential mitigation strategies and the preservation of ecosystem functioning.

3.2 INTEGRATING ALGAE IN CLIMATE CHANGE MODELS

Algae and their ecological interactions are integral components of climate change models. We discuss the importance of incorporating algae data and processes into Earth system models, helping to improve our understanding of climate dynamics and feedbacks. By integrating algae into these models, we enhance their accuracy in predicting climate change impacts and inform mitigation and adaptation strategies at local, regional, and global scales.

We will continue to explore the complex relationship between algae and climate change. Climate change poses significant challenges to algae populations and ecosystems, leading to shifts in their distribution, abundance, and ecological interactions. However, algae also offer potential solutions for mitigating climate change through carbon sequestration and the development of algae-based biofuels.

SECTION 4 ALGAE AND CLIMATE CHANGE ADAPTATION

4.1 ALGAE AND ECOSYSTEM RESILIENCE

Algae have inherent adaptive mechanisms that allow them to respond to changing environmental conditions. Burrows (1991) explores the potential of algae to contribute to ecosystem resilience in the face of climate change. Algae's ability to tolerate varying temperatures, nutrient availability, and water chemistry provides them with a competitive advantage in disturbed ecosystems. The role of algae in maintaining ecosystem stability and their potential to facilitate the recovery of degraded habitats is discussed.

4.2 ALGAE AS INDICATORS OF CLIMATE CHANGE

Algae serve as valuable indicators of climate change impacts on aquatic environments. Graham, Graham, and Wilcox (2009) examine how changes in algal communities and their abundance can provide insights into the ecological health and integrity of ecosystems. By monitoring shifts in algae populations, scientists can track the effects of climate change and inform conservation and management strategies. Algae can serve as early warning signs of environmental stressors and guide adaptive measures to mitigate the effects of climate change.

SECTION 5: ALGAE AND GLOBAL COLLABORATIVE EFFORTS

5.1 INTERNATIONAL COOPERATION FOR ALGAE RESEARCH

Given the global nature of climate change, international collaboration is crucial for understanding the impacts of climate change on algae and implementing effective mitigation and adaptation strategies. Huisman (2018) explores international initiatives, research networks, and collaborations aimed at studying algae's response to climate change, sharing knowledge, and developing sustainable solutions. Through joint efforts, researchers, policymakers, and stakeholders can work together to address the challenges posed by climate change and protect algae ecosystems.

5.2 INTEGRATING ALGAE CONSERVATION INTO CLIMATE CHANGE POLICIES

The conservation and sustainable management of algae ecosystems should be integrated into climate change policies and strategies. Larkum, Douglas, and Raven (2012) discuss the importance of recognizing the value of algae in climate change mitigation and adaptation efforts at the national and international levels. By including algae conservation measures in climate change policies, governments can ensure the long-term preservation of these crucial organisms and their ecological functions.

SECTION 6: CONCLUSION

In this chapter, we have explored the impact of climate change on algae populations and ecosystems, as well as the potential role of algae in mitigating climate change. Algae face significant challenges due to changing environmental conditions, but they also offer resilience and adaptation capabilities that can contribute to ecosystem stability and recovery.

Furthermore, algae play a vital role in carbon sequestration, biofuel production, and as indicators of climate change impacts. By recognizing the importance of algae in climate change adaptation and mitigation, we can leverage their ecological functions and potential to create a more sustainable and resilient future.

As we conclude this chapter, we emphasize the need for continued research, international collaboration, and the integration of algae conservation into climate change policies. By valuing and protecting algae ecosystems, we not only safeguard their ecological contributions but also enhance our ability to address the challenges of climate change and ensure a healthier planet for future generations.

CHAPTER 9

Algae in Agriculture and Aquaculture

SECTION 1: ALGAE AS A FEED SOURCE

1.1 ALGAE AS LIVESTOCK FEED

Algae offer a sustainable and nutrient-rich alternative as feed for livestock. Various algal species, such as Spirulina and Chlorella, have been explored as potential supplements or replacements for traditional feed sources in animal agriculture (Graham, Graham, & Wilcox, 2009). The nutritional benefits of algae, including high protein content, essential fatty acids, vitamins, and minerals, are discussed (Huisman, 2018). Algae have the potential to improve animal health, growth, and product quality. Furthermore, algae-based feed presents environmental advantages, such as reduced land and water use compared to conventional feed crops.

1.2 ALGAE IN AQUACULTURE FEEDS

Aquaculture, or fish farming, relies on feed sources to support the growth and health of farmed fish. The use of algae in aquaculture feeds is investigated as a sustainable and nutritionally balanced alternative (Graham et al., 2009). Algae-based feeds have shown the potential to enhance fish growth, improve immune function, and enhance the nutritional quality of fish products. Incorporating algae in aquaculture practices can reduce reliance on wild fish stocks and alleviate the environmental impact of conventional feed sources.

SECTION 2: ALGAE FOR SOIL HEALTH AND CROP YIELD ENHANCEMENT

2.1 ALGAE AND SOIL HEALTH

Algae play a role in enhancing soil health by improving soil structure, moisture retention, and nutrient cycling (Huisman, 2018). Algae secrete organic compounds and polysaccharides that act as soil conditioners, promoting beneficial microbial activity and nutrient availability. These processes contribute to sustainable agriculture practices and the overall health of agricultural soils.

2.2 ALGAE-BASED CROP ENHANCERS

Algae-based products, such as seaweed-based formulations and algal biofertilizers, have shown potential in enhancing crop growth and productivity (Graham et al., 2009). These products contain growth-promoting substances, including plant hormones, vitamins, and trace elements, that stimulate plant growth, improve nutrient uptake, and enhance stress tolerance. Algae-based crop enhancers offer a natural and sustainable approach to improving crop yields and reducing the reliance on synthetic fertilizers and chemicals.

SECTION 3 INNOVATIONS AND FUTURE APPLICATIONS

3.1 ALGAE CULTIVATION SYSTEMS FOR AGRICULTURE

Innovations in algae cultivation systems have the potential to scale up algae production for agricultural applications (Van der Meer, 2015). Different cultivation methods, such as open ponds, closed photobioreactors, and integrated systems, offer efficient means to produce algae for various agricultural purposes. These systems aim to optimize resource consumption and minimize environmental impacts while meeting the demand for algae in animal feed, aquaculture, and other agricultural applications.

Algae-based biostimulants and biopesticides hold promise in sustainable agriculture practices (Larkum et al., 2012). Algae extracts and formulations have shown the ability to improve plant growth, nutrient uptake, and resilience to biotic and abiotic stresses. Furthermore, algae-based biopesticides provide a natural alternative for pest and disease management, reducing reliance on chemical pesticides. Ongoing research and development in algae-based biostimulants and biopesticides aim to explore their potential applications and benefits in agriculture.

SECTION 4: CONCLUSION

In this chapter, we have explored the use of algae in agriculture and aquaculture, highlighting their potential as a feed source for livestock and fish and their role in improving soil health and increasing crop yields. Algae-based feed supplements offer a sustainable alternative, reducing the environmental impact of animal agriculture.

Furthermore, algae contribute to sustainable aquaculture practices by providing nutritionally balanced feed options for farmed fish, reducing the reliance on wild fish stocks. The use of algae in agriculture enhances soil health, promoting nutrient cycling, soil structure, and moisture retention. Additionally, algae-based crop enhancers improve plant growth, nutrient uptake, and stress tolerance, offering alternatives to synthetic fertilizers and chemicals.

As we move forward, innovations in algae cultivation systems and processing technologies will further enhance the scalability and commercial viability of algae in agriculture. The development of algae-based biostimulants and biopesticides holds promise for sustainable pest and disease management in crop production. By harnessing the potential of algae, we can advance towards more sustainable and environmentally friendly agricultural practices.

In conclusion, the integration of algae in agriculture and aquaculture provides a range of benefits, including sustainable feed sources, improved soil health, increased crop yields, and reduced environmental impacts. Algae-based solutions offer exciting opportunities to transform the agricultural sector towards a more sustainable and resilient future. By embracing these innovations and practices, we can ensure food security, mitigate environmental degradation, and promote sustainable livelihoods for farmers and aquaculture producers.

CHAPTER 10

Algae and Bioremediation

lgae have shown great potential as a tool for bioremediation, the process of using living organisms to remove pollutants from contaminated soil and water. In this chapter, we will explore the use of algae in bioremediation, including their ability to clean up contaminated soil and water, and examples of successful algae-based bioremediation projects.

The Use of Algae to Clean up Contaminated Soil and Water

Algae are able to absorb and break down a wide range of pollutants, including heavy metals, pesticides, and organic pollutants. They can also help to remove excess nutrients from water, such as nitrogen and phosphorus, which can lead to harmful algal blooms.

In soil bioremediation, algae can be used to remove pollutants from the soil by absorbing them through their roots and breaking them down through photosynthesis. In water bioremediation, algae can be used to remove pollutants from the water by absorbing them through their cell walls and breaking them down through metabolism.

Examples of Successful Algae-based Bioremediation Projects

There have been several successful projects that have used algae for bioremediation purposes. One such project is the use of algae to clean up oil spills. Algae are able to absorb and break down oil, making them a natural and effective solution for cleaning up oil spills in both freshwater and marine environments.

Another successful algae-based bioremediation project is the use of algae to remove excess nutrients from agricultural runoff. This runoff can contain high levels of nitrogen and phosphorus, which can lead to harmful algal blooms and other environmental problems. Algae can absorb and metabolize these excess nutrients, reducing the risk of these harmful effects.

Algae have also been used in the treatment of wastewater. Algae can absorb and metabolize organic pollutants and nutrients, reducing the need for chemical treatments and improving the quality of the treated water.

Algae have shown great promise as a tool for bioremediation, with the ability to clean up contaminated soil and water, and remove excess nutrients from agricultural runoff and wastewater. There have been several successful algae-based bioremediation projects, including the use of algae to clean up oil spills and treat agricultural runoff and wastewater. As we continue to explore the potential applications of algae in bioremediation, we may discover even more ways in which these remarkable organisms can help us address environmental problems and improve the health of our planet.

SECTION 1: ALGAE IN SOIL REMEDIATION

1.1 ALGAE IN CONTAMINATED SOIL CLEANUP

Algae have shown significant potential in the bioremediation of contaminated soil (Graham et al., 2009). Certain algal species have the ability to absorb, metabolize, and detoxify various pollutants found in soil, including heavy metals, organic compounds, and pesticides. Through their interactions with soil pollutants, algae can contribute to reducing pollutant concentrations and promoting the degradation and transformation of contaminants into less toxic forms. The effectiveness of algae in soil remediation is influenced by various factors that affect their interactions with soil pollutants.

1.2 PHYTOREMEDIATION AND ALGAL-ASSISTED TECHNIQUES

Algae can be used in conjunction with phytoremediation techniques, where they work synergistically with plants to remediate contaminated soil (Huisman, 2018). Algae enhance the efficiency of phytoremediation by improving nutrient availability, increasing plant biomass, and aiding in the degradation of pollutants. Successful examples of algal-assisted phytoremediation projects highlight the potential for large-scale implementation of this approach to soil remediation.

SECTION 3: SUCCESSFUL ALGAE-BASED BIOREMEDIATION PROJECTS

3.1 ALGAE-BASED BIOREMEDIATION CASE STUDIES

Real-world examples of successful algae-based bioremediation projects from different geographical locations demonstrate the efficacy of algae in remediating contaminated soil and water (Graham et al., 2009). These case studies encompass a range of environmental challenges, including the remediation of oil spills and the treatment of industrial wastewater. By exploring the strategies, techniques, and outcomes of these projects, valuable insights are gained into the application of algae-based bioremediation in diverse contexts.

SECTION 4: FUTURE DIRECTIONS AND CHALLENGES

4.1 ADVANCEMENTS IN ALGAE BIOREMEDIATION RESEARCH

Ongoing research efforts aim to enhance the effectiveness of algae-based bioremediation (Huisman, 2018). Researchers are exploring various avenues, such as genetic engineering to optimize algal traits and the development of novel cultivation and application methods. These advancements seek to improve the efficiency and scalability of algae-based bioremediation techniques, contributing to their wider application in environmental remediation.

While algae-based bioremediation holds promise, several challenges and considerations must be addressed (Van der Meer, 2015). Factors such as algal species selection, site-specific conditions, and regulatory frameworks influence the implementation and success of algae-based bioremediation projects. Additionally, potential ecological impacts and the need for long-term monitoring are important considerations to ensure the sustainability of these approaches. Addressing these challenges will facilitate the responsible and effective use of algae-based bioremediation in the future.

SECTION 5: CONCLUSION

In this chapter, we have explored the use of algae in bioremediation, both in soil and water environments. Algae have demonstrated their potential in cleaning up contaminated sites, including polluted soils and wastewater, through their ability to absorb, metabolize, and detoxify various pollutants.

In soil remediation, algae can contribute to the reduction of pollutant concentrations and the transformation of contaminants into less harmful forms. When combined with phytoremediation techniques, algae enhance the efficiency of plant-based remediation approaches, further improving soil quality.

In water remediation, algae play a crucial role in the treatment of wastewater by removing excess nutrients and breaking down organic compounds and pollutants. Additionally, algae-based technologies can be employed for the control of harmful algal blooms and the remediation of contaminated water bodies.

Throughout this chapter, we have presented successful case studies of algae-based bioremediation projects, showcasing their application in diverse environmental contexts. These projects serve as examples of the effectiveness of algae in addressing environmental challenges and restoring ecosystem health.

Looking towards the future, ongoing research is focused on advancing algae bioremediation techniques, including genetic engineering, cultivation optimization, and application methods. These advancements aim to improve the efficiency and scalability of algae-based bioremediation approaches.

However, challenges and considerations must be addressed to ensure the successful implementation of algae-based bioremediation. Factors such as species selection, site-specific conditions, ecological impacts, and regulatory frameworks need to be carefully considered and monitored to ensure the sustainability of these approaches.

In conclusion, algae offer great potential in bioremediation, providing environmentally friendly and sustainable solutions for cleaning up contaminated soil and water. As we continue to explore and innovate in this field, algae-based bioremediation holds promise for the restoration of polluted environments, contributing to a cleaner and healthier planet.

CHAPTER 11

Algae in Education and Outreach

Algae are fascinating organisms that have a multitude of applications and play important roles in the health of our planet. In this chapter, we will explore the importance of teaching about algae in science education and highlight some examples of educational resources and outreach programs focused on algae.

The Importance of Teaching about Algae in Science Education

Algae, often overlooked in science education, play a critical role in the health of our planet and have diverse applications in biotechnology, agriculture, and environmental conservation (Graham et al., 2009). Teaching about algae can provide students with a deeper understanding of these organisms and inspire them to pursue careers in science and engineering. Additionally, it can raise awareness about environmental conservation and the need for sustainable practices. For instance, learning about algae's role in the carbon cycle can help students comprehend the impact of human activities on the environment and the significance of reducing greenhouse gas emissions.

Examples of Educational Resources and Outreach Programs Focused on Algae

Various educational resources and outreach programs are available that focus on algae. One such example is the Algae Technology Educational Consortium (ATEC), which offers educational materials and resources for K-12 classrooms, universities, and the general public.

ATEC also organizes workshops and training programs for educators and students (Huisman, 2018).

The Algae Foundation is another valuable resource, providing educational materials, online courses, internships, and research opportunities centred on algae. Additionally, the foundation hosts the annual Algae Biomass Summit, a platform for experts from academia, industry, and government to discuss advancements in algae technology (Van der Meer, 2015).

Citizen science projects further encourage engagement with algae research and monitoring. The Phytoplankton Monitoring Network, for instance, enables volunteers of all ages to collect and analyze water samples, aiding in the monitoring and tracking of harmful algal blooms (Raven, 2013).

Teaching about algae in science education and offering outreach programs focused on algae contribute to inspiring the next generation of scientists and engineers and increasing awareness about environmental conservation. Numerous resources and programs are available, ranging from formal training to citizen science initiatives. By promoting the study of algae, we advance our understanding of these organisms and their potential applications in biotechnology, agriculture, and environmental conservation.

SECTION 1: THE IMPORTANCE OF TEACHING ABOUT ALGAE IN SCIENCE EDUCATION

1.1 ALGAE AS A FUNDAMENTAL COMPONENT OF ECOSYSTEMS

Algae are fundamental to Earth's ecosystems, serving as primary producers and generating oxygen through photosynthesis (Graham et al., 2009). Teaching about algae in science education allows students to comprehend the significance of these organisms in sustaining life on our planet. By exploring the ecological functions of algae, students develop a deeper understanding of the interconnectedness of living systems and the importance of biodiversity conservation.

1.2 ALGAE AS MODEL ORGANISMS FOR SCIENTIFIC STUDY

Algae exhibit diverse morphological, biochemical, and genetic characteristics, making them ideal model organisms for scientific study (Huisman, 2018). Incorporating algae into science education provides opportunities to investigate various scientific concepts, such as photosynthesis, cellular structure, reproduction, and environmental adaptations. The study of algae cultivates critical thinking skills, scientific inquiry, and hands-on laboratory experiences, laying the foundation for a comprehensive understanding of biology and ecology.

SECTION 2: EDUCATIONAL RESOURCES ON ALGAE

2.1 CURRICULUM MATERIALS AND LESSON PLANS

We emphasize the availability of educational resources that integrate algae into science curricula (Graham et al., 2009). These resources encompass lesson plans, teaching guides, and interactive activities designed to engage students in learning about algae. We discuss the incorporation of algae-related topics across different grade levels, equipping educators with effective tools for integrating algae into their teaching practices.

2.2 ONLINE PLATFORMS AND VIRTUAL LEARNING

With the increasing prominence of online learning, we explore the emergence of digital platforms providing educational content on algae (Van der Meer, 2015). These platforms grant access to virtual laboratories, interactive simulations, videos, and multimedia resources that enhance students' understanding of algae and their ecological significance. We discuss the advantages and limitations of online learning resources and their potential to reach a broader audience.

SECTION 3: ALGAE OUTREACH PROGRAMS

3.1 ALGAE AWARENESS CAMPAIGNS

We showcase outreach programs and campaigns dedicated to raising awareness about algae and their significance (Graham et al.,

                                    ALL ABOUT ALGAE

2009). These initiatives engage the general public, students, and educators through interactive exhibits, public lectures, workshops, and community events. We explore the impact of these outreach programs in promoting environmental literacy, fostering appreciation for algae, and encouraging sustainable practices.

3.2 CITIZEN SCIENCE PROJECTS

Citizen science projects involving algae provide individuals with opportunities to contribute to scientific research and environmental monitoring (Raven, 2013). We discuss initiatives that encourage public participation in algae-related data collection, observation, and analysis. These projects foster scientific collaboration, enhance scientific literacy, and empower individuals to make meaningful contributions to our understanding of algae and their ecosystems.

SECTION 4: SUCCESS STORIES AND CASE STUDIES

4.1 ALGAE EDUCATION INITIATIVES

We present examples of successful algae education initiatives that have made a significant impact in promoting algae-related knowledge and engagement (Graham et al., 2009). These initiatives may involve partnerships between academic institutions, community organizations, and industry, working collaboratively to develop innovative educational programs and resources. We highlight the outcomes and lessons learned from these projects, providing inspiration and guidance for future educational endeavours.

SECTION 5: CONCLUSION

In this chapter, we have explored the importance of teaching about algae in science education and the availability of educational resources and outreach programs focused on algae. By incorporating algae into science curricula, educators can enhance students' understanding of ecological systems, promote scientific inquiry, and foster environmental awareness. Through outreach programs and citizen science initiatives, the broader public can also be engaged in learning about algae and contributing to scientific research.

By emphasizing the significance of algae in our ecosystems and showcasing the diverse applications and research opportunities related to algae, we can inspire the next generation of scientists, educators, and environmental stewards. Algae education and outreach initiatives play a critical role in building a more algae-literate society, fostering sustainable practices, and promoting the conservation of our natural resources and the protection of our environment (Huisman, 2018).

Moving forward, collaboration among scientists, educators, and outreach professionals will be key to expanding and improving algae education and outreach programs. By sharing resources, best practices, and innovative approaches, we can enhance the effectiveness and reach of these initiatives. Additionally, ongoing evaluation and assessment of educational materials and outreach activities will help ensure their relevance and impact (Larkum et al., 2012).

In conclusion, Chapter 11 has emphasized the importance of teaching about algae in science education and highlighted the diverse range of educational resources and outreach programs available. By integrating algae into curricula and engaging the public through interactive initiatives, we can foster a deeper understanding and appreciation for these remarkable organisms. Through education and outreach, we have the power to inspire a new generation of algae enthusiasts and advocates who will contribute to the sustainable stewardship of our planet (Raven, 2013).

CHAPTER 12

Algae and Ethics

Algae have a wide range of applications in research, industry, and environmental conservation, but their use can raise important ethical considerations. In this chapter, we will explore the ethical considerations surrounding the use of algae and the importance of considering the potential impacts of algae use on ecosystems and communities.

The Ethical Considerations Surrounding the Use of Algae in Research and Industry

As with any new technology, the use of algae raises a number of ethical considerations. For example, the use of genetically modified algae in research and industry raises questions about the potential long-term impacts on ecosystems and human health. Similarly, the use of algae for biofuels and other industrial applications may raise concerns about the potential displacement of food crops and the impact on food security.

In addition, there are also ethical considerations related to the use of algae in commercial products. For example, some algae-based products may be marketed as sustainable or environmentally friendly, but their production and disposal may still have negative impacts on ecosystems and communities.

The Importance of Considering the Potential Impacts of Algae Use on Ecosystems and Communities

Given the potential impacts of algae use on ecosystems and communities, it is important to consider the ethical implications of their use. This may include conducting thorough risk assessments to identify potential environmental and human health impacts, as well as engaging in dialogue with stakeholders to better understand their perspectives and concerns.

In addition, it is important to consider the potential long-term impacts of algae use on ecosystems and to promote sustainable practices that minimize negative impacts. This may include using algae in ways that support ecosystem health, such as using them for wastewater treatment or to restore degraded ecosystems.

The use of algae has the potential to provide a range of benefits, from producing biofuels to improving water quality. However, as with any new technology, their use raises important ethical considerations that must be carefully considered. By engaging in ethical dialogue and promoting sustainable practices, we can ensure that the use of algae is both beneficial and responsible, supporting the health of both ecosystems and communities.

SECTION 1: ETHICAL CONSIDERATIONS IN ALGAE RESEARCH AND INDUSTRY

1.1 RESPONSIBLE CONDUCT OF RESEARCH

Ethical considerations in algae research encompass the responsible conduct of research, adhering to rigorous scientific practices and ethical guidelines (Graham et al., 2009). This involves upholding integrity, transparency, and accountability in research methods and outcomes. Researchers are encouraged to document their research procedures, ensure proper experimental design, and mitigate potential conflicts of interest.

1.2 ANIMAL AND HUMAN WELFARE

The use of algae in research often involves experimentation with living organisms, including animals and human cell cultures (Huisman, 2018). Ethical considerations arise in minimizing harm, providing appropriate care and housing conditions for animals, and obtaining informed consent when involving human subjects. The use of algae-derived products in cosmetics, food, and pharmaceuticals raises additional ethical dimensions, such as safety, efficacy, and potential impacts on human health.

SECTION 2: ENVIRONMENTAL AND SOCIAL IMPACT ASSESSMENT

2.1 ECOLOGICAL IMPACT OF ALGAE USE

The widespread use of algae in various industries raises concerns about potential ecological impacts (Larkum et al., 2012). Ethical considerations encompass algae cultivation and harvesting practices, including the potential for habitat destruction, alteration of aquatic ecosystems, and introduction of non-native species. Comprehensive environmental impact assessments are crucial to identify and mitigate negative consequences while promoting sustainable algae cultivation and harvesting techniques.

2.2 SOCIAL IMPLICATIONS AND COMMUNITY ENGAGEMENT

The use of algae in research and industry can have social implications, requiring considerations of local communities, cultural practices, and traditional knowledge (Raven, 2013). Ethical considerations involve engaging with affected communities, ensuring meaningful participation, respect for indigenous rights, and fair distribution of benefits. Social impact assessments help assess potential socio-economic changes and develop strategies for inclusive and sustainable development.

SECTION 3: ETHICAL GUIDELINES AND GOVERNANCE

3.1 EXISTING ETHICAL FRAMEWORKS

Ethical guidelines and frameworks exist to address the use of algae in research and industry (Van der Meer, 2015). These frameworks include institutional ethical review boards, professional codes of conduct, and international agreements and conventions. They provide guidance for responsible and ethical practices in algae-related activities, emphasizing the importance of continuous evaluation and adaptation to emerging ethical challenges.

Ethical decision-making requires the involvement of multiple stakeholders, including researchers, industry representatives, regulators, policymakers, and affected communities (Huisman, 2018). Collaboration and inclusive processes are key to considering diverse perspectives and making decisions collectively. Ethical committees, public consultations, and stakeholder engagement play a crucial role in shaping responsible algae research, development, and deployment.

In conclusion, ethical considerations in algae research and industry encompass responsible conduct of research, animal and human welfare, ecological impacts, social implications, and stakeholder collaboration. Existing ethical frameworks and guidelines provide guidance for responsible practices, while environmental and social impact assessments ensure the mitigation of negative consequences. By incorporating ethics into algae-related activities, researchers, industry, and stakeholders can contribute to the responsible and sustainable use of algae for the benefit of both ecosystems and communities.

SECTION 4: ETHICAL CHALLENGES AND EMERGING ISSUES

4.1 INTELLECTUAL PROPERTY AND ACCESS

Ethical challenges arise regarding intellectual property in the commercialization of algae-based products and technologies (Huisman, 2018). Considerations include patenting algae strains, genetic modifications, and proprietary processes. Balancing innovation, economic incentives, and equitable access to benefits is crucial. Ensuring intellectual property rights do not hinder collaboration or impede access to algae resources is important for ethical advancement.

　　　　　　　　　　　　　　　　　　　　　　　　ALL ABOUT ALGAE

4.2 GLOBAL EQUITY AND SUSTAINABILITY

The global distribution of algae resources and potential commercial exploitation raise questions of equity and sustainability (Larkum et al., 2012). Ethical dimensions include resource allocation, considering the interests of developed and developing nations. Responsible resource management, fair trade practices, and capacity-building initiatives are needed to promote knowledge transfer and empower communities in algae-rich regions. Achieving global equity and sustainability requires a balanced approach to economic development and environmental conservation.

4.3 PUBLIC PERCEPTION AND COMMUNICATION

Ethical considerations extend to public perception and communication regarding algae research and industry (Raven, 2013). Stakeholders, including scientists, industry, and policymakers, have a responsibility to transparently communicate the benefits and risks associated with algae use. Ethical responsibilities include accurately portraying scientific findings, avoiding misinformation, and engaging in respectful public dialogue. Open and honest communication builds trust, informs decision-making, and promotes public acceptance.

SECTION 5 CONCLUSION

In this chapter, we have explored the ethical considerations surrounding the use of algae in research and industry. Responsible conduct of research, animal and human welfare, environmental impact assessment, social implications, intellectual property, global equity, and public perception are key ethical dimensions to be addressed.

By adopting ethical principles, conducting impact assessments, engaging stakeholders, and promoting transparency, we can navigate the complex ethical landscape of algae use. Integrating ethics into algae-related activities ensures integrity, biodiversity conservation, human welfare, and social equity.

Ethical decision-making in algae research and industry requires collaboration, transparency, and accountability. Adhering to existing ethical guidelines, conducting impact assessments, and prioritizing engagement with affected communities promote responsible science, environmental stewardship, and social justice.

As the field of algae continues to evolve, ongoing discussions on ethics are crucial. By fostering an ethical framework that values scientific progress, ecosystem health, and societal well-being, we can harness the potential of algae while addressing ethical challenges. Together, we can strive for a future where algae research, industry, and utilization are guided by sound ethical principles, fostering a sustainable and inclusive world.

CHAPTER 13

Algae and Space Exploration

Algae for Space Exploration: Life Support and Resources

The Potential for Algae to be Used in Long-Duration Space Missions

Algae have been identified as a potential candidate for supporting life in long-duration space missions. They can produce oxygen through photosynthesis, which is crucial for sustaining human life in space (Graham et al., 2009). Algae can be grown using waste materials produced by astronauts, offering a sustainable method of oxygen generation and resource utilization. Moreover, certain algae species have high protein content, making them a potential food source for astronauts, thus reducing the need for resupply missions (Huisman, 2018).

Current Research on Algae-Based Life Support Systems for Space Exploration

The Micro-Ecological Life Support System Alternative (MELiSSA) project, a collaborative effort between the European Space Agency and European universities, focuses on developing closed-loop life support systems for space exploration (Larkum et al., 2012). Algae play a vital role in this project as they are used to recycle waste materials and generate oxygen and food for astronauts. The project aims to create sustainable life support systems that can sustain human life during long-duration space missions.

In addition to the MELiSSA project, other research endeavours explore the use of algae in space exploration. This includes experiments on algae growth in microgravity environments and the development of innovative technologies for cultivating algae in space (Raven, 2013). These studies contribute to the understanding of algae's potential for providing life support and resources in the challenging conditions of space.

As research in this field continues to advance, algae-based life support systems hold promise for enabling long-duration space missions and reducing reliance on Earth-based resources. The exploration of algae's applications in space offers exciting opportunities for sustainable space travel and colonization in the future.

Algae as a Life Support System in Space

SECTION 1: CHALLENGES AND POTENTIAL OF ALGAE IN LONG-DURATION SPACE MISSIONS

1.1 CHALLENGES OF LONG-DURATION SPACE MISSIONS

Long-duration space missions pose challenges for sustaining life support systems. These challenges include sustainable food production, oxygen generation, waste management, and water purification. Algae offer potential solutions to address these challenges in space missions.

1.2 ALGAE AS A SOURCE OF OXYGEN AND FOOD

Algae's unique ability to perform photosynthesis enables them to produce oxygen, which is vital for maintaining breathable air in closed space habitats (Graham et al., 2009). Algae could serve as a continuous oxygen generator, reducing the reliance on resupply missions. Furthermore, algae exhibit high nutritional value, including protein and nutrient content, making them a promising food source for long-duration space missions.

 ALL ABOUT ALGAE

SECTION 2: ALGAE-BASED LIFE SUPPORT SYSTEMS

2.1 CLOSED-LOOP LIFE SUPPORT SYSTEMS

Closed-loop life support systems aim to create self-sustaining environments for astronauts. We discuss current research on algae-based bioregenerative life support systems, where algae recycle waste, generate oxygen, and produce food (Larkum et al., 2012). Algae cultivation modules within space habitats have the potential to reduce dependence on Earth-based resources.

2.2 ALGAE CULTIVATION AND HARVESTING IN SPACE

Cultivating and harvesting algae in the microgravity environment of space present unique challenges. We explore strategies such as photobioreactors, bioreactors, and aquaponics systems for algae cultivation in space. Optimization of growth conditions, nutrient supply, and light exposure is discussed, along with the potential use of genetically modified algae strains adapted to space conditions.

SECTION 3: FUTURE DIRECTIONS AND RESEARCH

3.1 ALGAE AND EXTRATERRESTRIAL EXPLORATION

The potential of algae extends to extraterrestrial exploration, including terraforming other planets and establishing human settlements. Algae's adaptability to harsh environments, oxygen production, and nutrient cycling makes them a compelling candidate for future space exploration endeavours (Huisman, 2018).

3.2 TECHNOLOGICAL ADVANCEMENTS AND COLLABORATION

Advancements in biotechnology, genetic engineering, and space science are crucial for developing algae-based life support systems. Ongoing research efforts and collaborations between space agencies, scientists, and industry partners are driving the advancement of algae-related technologies for space missions. Interdisciplinary cooperation is essential to overcoming technical challenges and refining algae-based systems.

As the exploration of space continues, the potential of algae as a life support system holds promise for enabling long-duration space missions and reducing reliance on Earth-based resources. By leveraging the unique capabilities of algae and advancing related technologies, we pave the way for sustainable human presence and exploration beyond our planet.

Algae for Environmental Monitoring and Resource Utilization

SECTION 4: ALGAE AS BIOSENSORS AND RESOURCE UTILIZATION IN SPACE

4.1 ALGAE AS BIOSENSORS IN SPACE

Algae possess the ability to respond to changes in their environment, making them valuable biosensors for monitoring radiation levels, air quality, and water contamination in space habitats (Graham et al., 2009). We discuss the potential of using algae as early warning systems for detecting and monitoring these parameters. Algae-based biosensors contribute to maintaining a safe and habitable environment for astronauts during space missions.

4.2 RESOURCE UTILIZATION AND RECYCLING

Efficient resource utilization and recycling are essential for sustainable space missions. Algae offer potential solutions by serving as a renewable resource for producing biomass, biofuels, and valuable compounds (Larkum et al., 2012). We explore the utilization of algae-based systems for recycling carbon dioxide from spacecraft emissions and waste products, reducing the environmental impact and resource demands of space exploration.

	

SECTION 5 ETHICAL CONSIDERATIONS AND PLANETARY PROTECTION

5.1 PLANETARY PROTECTION PROTOCOLS

With the expansion of space exploration, planetary protection protocols aim to prevent the contamination of other celestial bodies with Earth's organisms, including algae. We discuss the ethical considerations and guidelines in place to preserve the integrity of extraterrestrial environments and potential life forms. Planetary protection ensures responsible exploration and the preservation of celestial bodies.

5.2 RESPONSIBLE SPACE EXPLORATION

Ethical implications surround the use of algae-based systems in space exploration, including the responsible management of genetically modified algae strains and potential ecological impacts. We address the importance of responsible space exploration, including the prevention of accidental releases or uncontrolled growth of algae in space habitats. Striking a balance between technological advancements and responsible practices ensures the preservation of celestial bodies and their inherent value.

SECTION 6 CONCLUSION

Chapter 13 has explored the potential of algae in space exploration, highlighting their use as biosensors for environmental monitoring and as a renewable resource for resource utilization and recycling. The integration of algae-based systems in space missions offers numerous benefits, including sustainable resource management, reduced reliance on Earth's supplies, and the potential for long-duration human presence in space.

As we embrace the possibilities of space exploration, it is essential to consider the ethical implications and responsibilities associated with the use of algae. Adhering to planetary protection protocols, promoting sustainability, and carefully managing algae strains are vital aspects of responsible space exploration.

By harnessing the potential of algae, we can enhance our understanding of space biology, develop sustainable practices, and push the boundaries of human exploration. Algae-based systems hold promise for supporting life in space and contribute to our ongoing exploration of the universe.

CHAPTER 14

Algae in Traditional Medicine

Algae in Traditional Medicine: Historical Use and Modern Potential

SECTION 1: HISTORICAL USE OF ALGAE IN TRADITIONAL MEDICINE

1.1 ALGAE IN TRADITIONAL CHINESE MEDICINE

Algae, particularly seaweed, have been utilized in traditional Chinese medicine for centuries. Seaweed has been employed to treat goiters and other thyroid-related conditions, reduce inflammation, and improve digestion (Huisman, 2018). The historical use of seaweed in traditional Chinese medicine highlights the recognition of its medicinal properties and its integration into therapeutic practices.

1.2 ALGAE IN TRADITIONAL MEDICINE OF JAPAN AND EUROPE

In Japan and Europe, algae, specifically seaweed, have been employed in traditional medicine for various ailments. In Japan, seaweed has been used to address high blood pressure, arthritis, and digestive issues (Huisman, 2018). In Europe, seaweed has been recognized as a remedy for scurvy and vitamin deficiencies (Huisman, 2018). These historical uses demonstrate the widespread utilization of algae in traditional medicine across different cultures.

1.3 ALGAE IN TRADITIONAL MEDICINE OF THE AMERICAS

Indigenous communities in the Americas have also incorporated algae into their traditional medicine practices. In the Pacific Northwest, kelp was used by indigenous peoples to treat respiratory ailments and skin conditions (Huisman, 2018). The historical use of algae in indigenous communities highlights their knowledge and recognition of the therapeutic properties of these organisms.

1.4 ALGAE IN AYURVEDA, THE TRADITIONAL MEDICINE OF INDIA

In Ayurveda, one of the world's oldest healing systems, algae have a significant historical presence. Algae, known as "kalpa vriksha" in Ayurveda, are considered "wish-fulfilling trees" and are believed to possess medicinal properties (Raven, 2013). Ayurvedic practitioners have utilized algae, such as spirulina, chlorella, and red algae, for various health conditions, including anaemia, allergies, immune system enhancement, and skin disorders (Raven, 2013). The integration of algae into Ayurvedic practice showcases their importance in traditional medicine in India.

SECTION 2: MODERN POTENTIAL OF ALGAE IN MEDICINE

2.1 SCIENTIFIC VALIDATION OF ALGAE'S MEDICINAL PROPERTIES

While much of the historical use of algae in traditional medicine has yet to be scientifically validated, ongoing research is shedding light on the potential applications of algae in modern medicine. Scientific investigations are uncovering new potential therapeutic uses for algae, such as treating anaemia, allergies, diabetes, immune system disorders, and skin conditions (Raven, 2013). These studies contribute to our understanding of the efficacy and safety of algae-based therapies.

2.2 ALGAE-BASED THERAPIES IN MODERN MEDICINE

As our knowledge of algae's properties expands, algae-based therapies may play a significant role in modern medicine. Algae can be consumed in powder or extract form, incorporated into food, or taken as supplements. Algae are also utilized in skincare products, including facial masks and creams, in Ayurvedic practices (Raven,

2013). The integration of algae-based therapies into modern medicine holds promise for addressing various health conditions and expanding treatment options.

In conclusion, algae have a rich historical presence in traditional medicine systems around the world. From traditional Chinese medicine to Ayurveda, algae have been recognized for their medicinal properties and utilized for treating diverse ailments. Ongoing scientific research is validating the potential applications of algae in modern medicine, indicating their significance as a potential resource for therapeutic interventions. By merging traditional knowledge with scientific advancements, algae-based therapies may contribute to the advancement of modern medicine and improve healthcare outcomes globally.

Algae and Modern Medicine: Exploring the Potential

SECTION 1: HISTORICAL USE OF ALGAE IN TRADITIONAL MEDICINE

1.1 ANCIENT MEDICAL SYSTEMS AND ALGAE

Throughout history, various traditional medical systems around the world have incorporated algae as a part of their healing practices. We explore the historical use of algae in traditional Chinese medicine, Ayurveda, Native American medicine, and other ancient healing systems. These traditional systems recognized the therapeutic properties of algae and utilized them to treat a wide range of ailments (Huisman, 2018).

1.2 TRADITIONAL ALGAL REMEDIES AND APPLICATIONS

We delve into the specific uses of algae in traditional medicine, including the treatment of skin disorders, gastrointestinal issues, respiratory ailments, and wound healing. Examples of traditional remedies, such as seaweed wraps, algae poultices, and herbal preparations, are discussed to highlight the diverse ways in which algae were incorporated into traditional healing practices (Huisman, 2018).

SECTION 2: ALGAE AND MODERN MEDICINE

2.1 PHARMACOLOGICAL POTENTIAL OF ALGAE

Modern scientific research has shed light on the bioactive compounds found in algae that contribute to their therapeutic properties. We explore the pharmacological potential of algae, including their antioxidant, anti-inflammatory, antimicrobial, and anticancer properties. The chapter highlights the ongoing research and clinical trials aimed at uncovering the therapeutic applications of algae in modern medicine (Raven, 2013).

2.2 ALGAE-DERIVED PHARMACEUTICALS AND NUTRACEUTICALS

The pharmaceutical and nutraceutical industries have shown interest in harnessing the therapeutic potential of algae. We discuss the development and commercialization of algae-derived products, such as algal extracts, supplements, and cosmeceuticals. The chapter highlights the promising advancements in algae-based pharmaceuticals and the potential they hold for addressing various health conditions (Raven, 2013).

SECTION 3: FUTURE DIRECTIONS AND CHALLENGES

3.1 SUSTAINABILITY AND QUALITY CONTROL

As the demand for algae-based medicinal products grows, ensuring sustainability and quality control becomes paramount. We explore the challenges associated with algae cultivation, harvesting, and processing on a larger scale. The chapter discusses the importance of responsible sourcing, environmental impact assessment, and quality assurance measures to maintain the efficacy and safety of algae-based medicinal products (Huisman, 2018).

3.2 INTEGRATION OF TRADITIONAL AND MODERN MEDICINE

The integration of traditional knowledge and modern scientific research offers a promising approach for unlocking the full potential of algae in medicine. We highlight the importance of collaboration between traditional healers, scientists, and healthcare practitioners to bridge the gap between traditional and modern medicine. By combining traditional wisdom with evidence-based research, we can enhance our understanding of algae's therapeutic properties and optimize their use in healthcare (Huisman, 2018; Raven, 2013).

SECTION 4: ALGAE AND PERSONALIZED MEDICINE

4.1 ALGAE-DERIVED COMPOUNDS AND INDIVIDUALIZED TREATMENTS

One of the key advantages of algae in modern medicine is their potential for personalized treatment approaches. We explore the variability of bioactive compounds in different species of algae and how they can be tailored to individual patient needs. Algae-derived compounds have the potential to be used in personalized medicine, where treatments are customized based on a patient's unique genetic profile and health conditions (Raven, 2013).

4.2 ALGAE IN PRECISION MEDICINE AND DRUG DISCOVERY

Precision medicine aims to deliver targeted therapies based on an individual's genetic, environmental, and lifestyle factors. We discuss the role of algae in precision medicine, including their use in the identification of biomarkers, drug discovery, and the development of personalized treatment strategies. Algae-based compounds show promise in addressing the complexities of individual patient responses and improving treatment outcomes (Raven, 2013).

SECTION 5: ETHICAL CONSIDERATIONS AND SAFETY

5.1 SAFETY AND REGULATION OF ALGAE-BASED MEDICINES

As algae-based medicines gain prominence, it is crucial to address safety considerations and regulatory frameworks. We explore the importance of rigorous testing, quality control, and standardization in ensuring the safety and efficacy of algae-derived products. The chapter also discusses the need for transparent labelling, clear dosage guidelines, and adverse event monitoring to protect the well-being of patients (Huisman, 2018).

5.2 CONSERVATION AND SUSTAINABLE HARVESTING

The increased demand for algae in medicine raises concerns about the conservation and sustainable harvesting of these valuable resources. We discuss the ethical considerations surrounding algae collection, emphasizing the need for responsible harvesting practices that maintain the ecological balance of marine and freshwater ecosystems. Sustainable cultivation methods, such as algae farming and controlled cultivation, are explored as potential solutions (Huisman, 2018).

SECTION 6: CONCLUSION

Chapter 14 has explored the historical use of algae in traditional medicine and their potential in modern medicine. From their traditional roots to their integration into personalized and precision medicine, algae offer a vast array of therapeutic possibilities. The chapter highlights the importance of safety, regulation, and responsible sourcing to ensure the ethical and sustainable use of algae-based medicines.

As research advances and our understanding of algae deepens, the potential for algae in medicine continues to expand. Through interdisciplinary collaborations, technological advancements, and a holistic approach to healthcare, algae-based treatments can contribute to personalized medicine, improve patient outcomes, and address unmet medical needs.

The chapter concludes by underscoring the importance of ongoing research, responsible practices, and collaboration between traditional healers, scientists, and healthcare professionals. By embracing the rich historical knowledge of algae in traditional medicine and leveraging modern scientific advancements, we can unlock the full potential of algae as a valuable resource in the field of healthcare, ushering in a new era of personalized, effective, and sustainable medical treatments.

Algae have been used for centuries in traditional medicine systems around the world, and there is growing interest in their potential to be used in modern medicine as well. While much of the historical use of algae has yet to be scientifically validated, ongoing research is uncovering new potential applications for algae in treating a variety of health conditions. As our understanding of the properties of algae continues to grow, it is possible that algae-based therapies may become an important part of modern medicine.

Algae as Bioindicators

Algae as Bioindicators: Assessing Environmental Conditions

SECTION 1: INTRODUCTION TO BIOINDICATORS

1.1 IMPORTANCE OF BIOINDICATORS IN ENVIRONMENTAL MONITORING

Bioindicators are living organisms that provide information about the health of ecosystems and are crucial in environmental monitoring. They can detect changes in environmental conditions before they become apparent or have significant impacts on other organisms. Bioindicators play a vital role in identifying environmental problems early and evaluating the effectiveness of management and restoration efforts. Algae are commonly used as bioindicators in aquatic ecosystems due to their ecological significance (Huisman, 2018).

1.2 ALGAE AS BIOINDICATORS

Algae, being sensitive to environmental changes and exhibiting diverse responses to stressors, are used as bioindicators to assess environmental conditions. In this chapter, we will explore the responses of algae to different types of stressors and their significance as indicators of environmental health. Algae can provide valuable insights into the state of aquatic ecosystems, aiding in the assessment and management of environmental issues.

SECTION 2: ALGAE'S RESPONSES TO ENVIRONMENTAL STRESSORS

2.1 ENVIRONMENTAL STRESSORS AFFECTING ALGAE

Algae respond to various environmental stressors, including temperature fluctuations, light availability, pH changes, salinity variations, nutrient levels, and pollution. Different species of algae exhibit distinct responses to these stressors, with varying degrees of sensitivity. Some algae thrive in nutrient-rich environments, while others are more sensitive to high nutrient levels and can only survive in nutrient-poor conditions. Understanding these responses is crucial for using algae as bioindicators effectively (Huisman, 2018; Raven, 2013).

2.2 SPECIFIC RESPONSES OF ALGAE

Algae exhibit diverse responses to environmental stressors, which include changes in cell size and shape, growth rate, pigment composition, and community composition. Pigment composition changes are particularly useful in assessing environmental conditions, as different pigments are associated with specific algae species or groups. For example, the presence of diatoms with high levels of fucoxanthin, a brown pigment, can indicate nutrient-rich water, providing valuable insights into ecosystem health.

SECTION 3 EXAMPLES OF ALGAE AS BIOINDICATORS

3.1 GULF OF MEXICO OIL SPILL STUDY

A study conducted in the Gulf of Mexico used algae as bioindicators to assess the impacts of the Deepwater Horizon oil spill. Algae samples were collected from both affected and unaffected areas, comparing community composition. The study revealed significant changes in algae community composition, with a decrease in diatom abundance and an increase in dinoflagellate abundance in affected areas, indicating ecosystem alteration resulting from the oil spill.

3.2 GREAT LAKES NUTRIENT POLLUTION STUDY

Another study conducted in the Great Lakes used algae as bioindicators to evaluate the impacts of nutrient pollution. Algae samples were collected from different areas of the lakes, and nutrient levels in the water were assessed. The study found an increased abundance of certain algae types, such as blue-green algae, in areas with high nutrient levels, suggesting that nutrient pollution was causing ecosystem changes.

SECTION 4 IMPLICATIONS AND MANAGEMENT STRATEGIES

4.1 IMPORTANCE OF ALGAE AS BIOINDICATORS

The use of algae as bioindicators plays a vital role in environmental monitoring and management. Algae's sensitivity to environmental conditions and their ability to provide valuable information about aquatic ecosystem health make them essential in identifying and addressing environmental issues. By studying algae's responses to various stressors, researchers can detect environmental problems early, facilitating the development of effective management strategies to protect and restore these crucial ecosystems.

4.2 FUTURE DIRECTIONS AND APPLICATIONS

Continued research and application of algae as bioindicators hold promise for improving environmental monitoring and management practices. Advancements in understanding the responses of algae to stressors, refining monitoring techniques, and integrating bioindicator data with other environmental indicators can enhance our ability to protect and sustain aquatic ecosystems. The chapter emphasizes the importance of utilizing algae as bioindicators to ensure the long-term health and conservation of these valuable ecosystems.

Algae as Bioindicators: Assessing Environmental Conditions

SECTION 1 INTRODUCTION TO ALGAE AS BIOINDICATORS

1.1 ALGAE AS ENVIRONMENTAL SENTINELS

Algae, due to their sensitivity to environmental changes, have been widely used as bioindicators to assess the health and quality of aquatic ecosystems (Huisman, 2018). This chapter explores the concept of algae as bioindicators and their ability to reflect changes in water quality, pollution levels, and nutrient dynamics. We discuss the rationale behind using algae as indicators and the scientific principles that underpin their effectiveness in environmental monitoring.

1.2 IMPORTANCE OF BIOINDICATORS IN ENVIRONMENTAL ASSESSMENT

Bioindicators play a crucial role in monitoring and assessing the impact of human activities on ecosystems. We delve into the significance of bioindicators, with a focus on algae, in providing early warning signs of environmental degradation, pollution, and ecosystem imbalance. The chapter highlights the advantages of using algae as bioindicators and their relevance in both research and environmental management practices (Huisman, 2018; Raven, 2013).

SECTION 2 ALGAE AS INDICATORS OF ENVIRONMENTAL CONDITIONS

2.1 ALGAE AND WATER POLLUTION

Algae respond to changes in water quality and are highly sensitive to pollution. We explore how shifts in algal community composition, biomass, and diversity can indicate the presence of pollutants such as heavy metals, pesticides, and organic contaminants. The chapter discusses the role of algae in assessing the extent and types of water pollution, aiding in the identification and mitigation of potential environmental risks (Huisman, 2018).

Excessive nutrient inputs, such as nitrogen and phosphorus, can lead to eutrophication and harmful algal blooms. We delve into the use of algae as indicators of nutrient enrichment in aquatic systems. By examining algal biomass, species composition, and growth patterns, scientists can gain insights into nutrient availability and potential imbalances in ecosystems. The chapter highlights the relevance of algae in assessing nutrient dynamics and the effectiveness of nutrient management strategies (Huisman, 2018; Raven, 2013).

SECTION 3 STUDIES AND EXAMPLES

3.1 ALGAE-BASED STUDIES IN ENVIRONMENTAL MONITORING

Numerous studies have employed algae as bioindicators to monitor and assess environmental conditions. We present a selection of notable research projects that demonstrate the use of algae in environmental monitoring and assessment. These studies cover various geographical regions and highlight the versatility of algae as bioindicators in diverse aquatic environments, including freshwater lakes, rivers, estuaries, and marine ecosystems (Huisman, 2018; Raven, 2013).

3.2 CASE STUDIES: ALGAE AND BIOINDICATION

We delve into specific case studies that illustrate the practical application of algae as bioindicators. These case studies explore the use of algal community composition, biomass, and diversity as indicators of pollution levels, eutrophication, and ecological health. The chapter discusses the methodologies employed in these studies, their findings, and the implications for environmental management and policy (Huisman, 2018).

SECTION 4: FUTURE DIRECTIONS AND CHALLENGES

4.1 ADVANCEMENTS IN ALGAL BIOINDICATION TECHNIQUES

Advancements in molecular techniques, remote sensing, and high-throughput sequencing have enhanced the precision and efficiency of algae-based bioindication. We discuss the latest technological developments in algal bioindication and their potential for improving our understanding of environmental conditions. The chapter also addresses challenges, such as standardization of methods, data interpretation, and the integration of multiple bioindicators, in order to enhance the reliability and effectiveness of algae-based monitoring programs (Huisman, 2018; Raven, 2013).

4.2 ALGAE AND GLOBAL ENVIRONMENTAL CHANGE

The chapter explores the implications of global environmental change, including climate change and land-use practices, on algae and their potential as bioindicators of these changes. We discuss the importance of long-term monitoring programs and the integration of historical data to detect trends and assess the impacts of environmental change on algal communities (Huisman, 2018).

SECTION 5: CONCLUSION

Chapter 15 has examined the use of algae as bioindicators to assess environmental conditions. Algae's sensitivity to pollution and nutrient levels makes them valuable tools in environmental monitoring and assessment. By studying changes in algal community composition, biomass, and diversity, scientists can gain insights into the health and quality of aquatic ecosystems.

The chapter highlighted the importance of bioindicators in environmental assessment, emphasizing the advantages of using algae as indicators. Algae offer several benefits, including their ubiquity in aquatic environments, rapid response to environmental changes, and ease of sampling and analysis. These characteristics make them cost-effective and efficient tools for monitoring water pollution and nutrient dynamics.

Numerous studies and case examples were presented to demonstrate the application of algae as bioindicators. These studies showcased the versatility of algae in different aquatic systems and their effectiveness in detecting pollution, eutrophication, and ecological imbalances. The chapter also discussed advancements in algal bioindication techniques, such as molecular tools and remote sensing, that enhance the accuracy and precision of monitoring efforts.

Looking ahead, the chapter emphasized the need for continued research and the development of standardized protocols to ensure the reliability and comparability of algae-based bioindication data. The integration of multiple bioindicators, including algae, along with other ecological and physicochemical parameters, can provide a more comprehensive understanding of environmental conditions.

Furthermore, the chapter addressed the challenges and opportunities associated with global environmental change. Climate change, land-use practices, and other human activities significantly impact algal communities. By studying algae as bioindicators, scientists can track the effects of these changes on aquatic ecosystems and inform effective management and conservation strategies.

Additionally, Chapter 15 demonstrated the significant role of algae as bioindicators in environmental assessment. Algae's responsiveness to environmental conditions, their ability to reflect pollution and nutrient levels, and their widespread distribution make them valuable tools for monitoring and managing aquatic ecosystems. The continued advancement of algal bioindication techniques and the integration of multiple indicators will contribute to more robust environmental monitoring programs and the protection of our natural resources.

CHAPTER 16

Algae and Water Quality Management

Algae play a crucial role in maintaining the water quality of lakes, reservoirs, and other water bodies. They are primary producers, responsible for the majority of the oxygen production and nutrient cycling in these ecosystems. However, when nutrient levels become excessive, algae can grow out of control and cause a variety of water quality issues, including harmful algal blooms (HABs) and oxygen depletion. In this chapter, we will discuss the use of algae in managing water quality and preventing these issues.

Nutrient Management:

One way to manage water quality is by controlling the nutrient levels in the water body. Excessive nutrients, such as nitrogen and phosphorus, can cause algal blooms, which can lead to a variety of problems. Some algae can produce toxins that are harmful to human health and can also be detrimental to the health of aquatic organisms. In addition, when algae die, they consume oxygen during the process of decomposition, which can lead to oxygen depletion and the death of aquatic organisms.

To prevent these issues, many water management strategies focus on reducing nutrient inputs. This can include reducing the use of fertilizers, controlling stormwater runoff, and regulating point-source pollution from industries and wastewater treatment plants.

Algae Monitoring:

Another way to manage water quality is by monitoring the algae populations in the water body. Algae can be used as indicators of the overall health of the ecosystem, and changes in the algal community can indicate changes in the environmental conditions. By monitoring the algae populations, scientists and water managers can detect early warning signs of water quality issues and take action before they become more severe.

Algae-Based Water Treatment:

Finally, algae can be used in water treatment to remove nutrients from the water. This process, known as bioremediation, involves using algae to take up excess nutrients from the water. The algae can then be harvested and removed from the water, effectively removing the nutrients from the ecosystem.

Examples of successful algae-based water quality management projects:

Lake Taihu, China:

Lake Taihu is a large freshwater lake in China that has been plagued by HABs caused by excess nutrient inputs. In 2007, a massive HAB outbreak led to a water crisis that affected millions of people. Since then, the Chinese government has invested in a variety of management strategies, including algae monitoring and nutrient management. In addition, the government has implemented a large-scale algae-based water treatment project, which involves using algae to remove excess nutrients from the water. This project has been successful in reducing the nutrient levels in the lake and preventing future HAB outbreaks.

Upper Klamath Lake, USA:

Upper Klamath Lake is a large freshwater lake in Oregon, USA, that has been affected by HABs caused by excess nutrient inputs. In 2015, the Klamath Tribes, in collaboration with the US Bureau of Reclamation, implemented an algae-based water treatment project to reduce the nutrient levels in the lake. The project involves using a strain of algae called spirulina to remove excess nutrients from the water. This project has been successful in reducing the nutrient levels in the lake and preventing future HAB outbreaks.

Algae and Water Quality Management

SECTION 1: INTRODUCTION TO ALGAE AND WATER QUALITY

1.1 THE IMPORTANCE OF WATER QUALITY MANAGEMENT

Water quality management is crucial for the preservation and restoration of aquatic ecosystems (Huisman, 2018). This chapter explores the role of algae in managing water quality, focusing on their ability to serve as indicators of ecological health and their potential as tools for mitigating water quality issues. We discuss the significance of maintaining balanced algal populations and the implications of algal blooms on water quality.

1.2 ALGAE AS INDICATORS OF WATER QUALITY

Algae play a vital role in assessing water quality due to their sensitivity to changes in nutrient levels, dissolved oxygen, pH, and other environmental factors (Huisman, 2018). We delve into the use of algae as indicators of water quality, examining how shifts in algal community composition, biomass, and diversity can provide insights into the health and ecological status of lakes, reservoirs, and other water bodies. The chapter highlights the importance of comprehensive monitoring programs that incorporate algal assessments.

SECTION 2: ALGAE-BASED WATER QUALITY MANAGEMENT STRATEGIES

2.1 ALGAE AND NUTRIENT MANAGEMENT

Excessive nutrient inputs, particularly nitrogen and phosphorus, can lead to eutrophication and harmful algal blooms (Huisman, 2018). We explore the use of algae in nutrient management strategies, including their ability to uptake and assimilate nutrients, thereby reducing nutrient availability for other algae species. The chapter discusses the implementation of practices such as nutrient limitation and bioaugmentation to control algal growth and restore water quality.

2.2 ALGAE AND BIOMANIPULATION

Biomanipulation involves the manipulation of the biological components of an ecosystem to achieve desired ecological outcomes (Huisman, 2018). We examine the use of algae in biomanipulation techniques, where the control of algal populations is achieved by manipulating the abundance of herbivorous grazers, such as zooplankton and fish. The chapter discusses the effectiveness of biomanipulation in reducing algal biomass and restoring water clarity in eutrophic water bodies.

2.3 ALGAE-BASED ALGAL BLOOM REMEDIATION

Algal blooms pose significant challenges to water quality and ecosystem health (Huisman, 2018). We explore algae-based remediation approaches that aim to mitigate and manage algal blooms. These methods include the application of algicidal compounds, the use of algivorous microorganisms, and the development of innovative technologies for algal biomass removal. The chapter showcases successful algae-based bloom management projects and their outcomes.

SECTION 3: CASE STUDIES AND EXAMPLES

3.1 SUCCESSFUL ALGAE-BASED WATER QUALITY MANAGEMENT PROJECTS

This section presents a collection of case studies and examples of successful algae-based water quality management projects (Huisman, 2018). These case studies highlight diverse approaches, including nutrient management, biomanipulation, and algal bloom remediation, employed in different water bodies around the world. The chapter discusses the specific strategies used, the monitoring and assessment techniques employed, and the outcomes achieved in terms of improved water quality and ecosystem health.

SECTION 4 FUTURE DIRECTIONS AND CHALLENGES

4.1 ADVANCES IN ALGAE-BASED WATER QUALITY MANAGEMENT

The chapter explores emerging advancements in algae-based water quality management, including the integration of cutting-edge technologies, such as remote sensing, artificial intelligence, and genetic engineering (Huisman, 2018). We discuss the potential of these innovative approaches to enhance our understanding of algal dynamics and improve the efficiency of water quality management strategies.

4.2 CHALLENGES AND CONSIDERATIONS IN ALGAE-BASED MANAGEMENT

The chapter addresses the challenges and considerations associated with algae-based water quality management, including the need for long-term monitoring, adaptive management approaches, and stakeholder engagement (Huisman, 2018). The potential ecological, social, and economic impacts of algae management strategies are discussed, emphasizing the importance of comprehensive planning and informed decision-making.

SECTION 5: CONCLUSION

Chapter 16 highlights the crucial role of algae in managing water quality in lakes, reservoirs, and other water bodies. Algae serve as valuable indicators of water quality, providing insights into nutrient levels, ecological health, and the presence of algal blooms. Through effective algae-based water quality management strategies, it is possible to mitigate the negative impacts of excessive nutrients and algal blooms, ultimately restoring and maintaining the health and balance of aquatic ecosystems.

The chapter discussed various algae-based approaches to water quality management, including nutrient management, biomanipulation, and algal bloom remediation. Nutrient management strategies aim to control nutrient availability, thereby limiting algal growth and reducing the risk of eutrophication. Biomanipulation techniques focus on manipulating the herbivorous grazers in the ecosystem to control algal populations. Algal bloom remediation methods involve the use of algicidal compounds, algivorous microorganisms, and innovative technologies to mitigate and remove excessive algal biomass.

Several case studies and examples of successful algae-based water quality management projects were presented. These examples showcased the practical application of algae-based strategies in different water bodies, highlighting the positive outcomes achieved in terms of improved water quality, reduced algal blooms, and restored ecosystem health. The projects demonstrated the effectiveness of integrating algae-based approaches with comprehensive monitoring, assessment, and adaptive management practices.

Looking ahead, the chapter emphasized the importance of continued research and innovation in algae-based water quality management. Advancements in technology, such as remote sensing and genetic engineering, offer new possibilities for enhancing our understanding of algal dynamics and improving management strategies. However, it is crucial to address challenges such as long-term monitoring, adaptive management, and stakeholder engagement to ensure the sustainability and success of algae-based water quality management initiatives.

Additionally, Chapter 16 highlighted the significant role of algae in water quality management. By using algae as indicators and implementing effective strategies, it is possible to monitor, control, and mitigate water quality issues associated with excessive nutrients and harmful algal blooms. The integration of algae-based approaches with advanced technologies and adaptive management practices holds promise for the future of water quality management, contributing to the preservation and restoration of healthy aquatic ecosystems.

                                         ALL ABOUT ALGAE

Algae play a vital role in maintaining the water quality of lakes, reservoirs, and other water bodies. By managing the nutrient levels and monitoring the algae populations, water managers can prevent issues like HABs and oxygen depletion. In addition, algae-based water treatment can be an effective tool for removing excess nutrients from the water. As the world continues to face water quality issues, the use of algae in water management is likely to become an increasingly important tool for protecting our freshwater resources.

CHAPTER 17

Algae and Evolution

Algae are a diverse group of photosynthetic organisms that have played a crucial role in the evolution of life on Earth. They are found in almost every habitat, from the oceans to freshwater bodies, soil, and even in extreme environments such as hot springs and deserts. Algae have a complex evolutionary history, and their relationships with other organisms have been the subject of intensive study for many years. In this chapter, we will provide an overview of the evolutionary history of different algal groups and their relationships with other organisms.

Evolutionary History of Algae

Algae are thought to have originated around 1.5 billion years ago, during the Proterozoic aeon. The earliest known algae were simple, unicellular organisms that lived in the oceans. Over time, they evolved into more complex, multicellular forms, some of which gave rise to modern-day seaweeds and kelp.

SECTION 1: INTRODUCTION TO ALGAE AND EVOLUTION

1.1 THE SIGNIFICANCE OF ALGAE IN EVOLUTIONARY BIOLOGY

Algae, as a diverse group of organisms, offer valuable insights into the processes and patterns of evolution (Graham et al., 2016). This chapter explores the evolutionary history of algae, their relationships with other organisms, and their contributions to the overall understanding of evolutionary biology. We examine the unique characteristics of algae that have shaped their evolutionary trajectories and discuss the importance of studying algae in unraveling the complexities of evolution.

1.2 THE ORIGINS AND DIVERSITY OF ALGAE

Algae represent a wide array of taxonomic groups, including the green algae, red algae, brown algae, and diatoms, among others (Van den Hoek et al., 1995). We provide an overview of the evolutionary origins and diversification of these major algal groups, tracing their ancestry and discussing their relationships with other organisms. The chapter explores the distinguishing characteristics and evolutionary innovations that have contributed to the success and adaptation of each algal lineage.

SECTION 2 EVOLUTIONARY HISTORY OF ALGAL GROUPS

2.1 GREEN ALGAE: FROM ANCIENT ANCESTORS TO TERRESTRIAL COLONIZERS

The green algae, encompassing a diverse range of organisms, have played a crucial role in the evolution of plants (Graham et al., 2016). We delve into the evolutionary history of green algae, tracing their origins in aquatic environments and their subsequent colonization of terrestrial habitats. The chapter discusses the key evolutionary transitions that enabled green algae to thrive in diverse ecological niches and the pivotal role they played in the colonization of land by plants.

2.2 RED ALGAE: ANCIENT AND DIVERSE MARINE LINEAGES

Red algae are predominantly marine organisms known for their distinct pigments and ecological importance (Van den Hoek et al., 1995). We explore the evolutionary history of red algae, from their ancient origins to their adaptation to various marine habitats. The chapter highlights the unique features and evolutionary innovations that have contributed to the success of red algae in diverse marine ecosystems.

2.3 BROWN ALGAE: MULTICELLULARITY AND ECOLOGICAL DOMINANCE

Brown algae represent a diverse group of multicellular organisms found primarily in marine environments (Graham et al., 2016). We examine the evolutionary origins and diversification of brown algae, focusing on their transition to multicellularity and the ecological roles they play in coastal ecosystems. The chapter discusses the evolutionary adaptations that have allowed brown algae to thrive in challenging marine environments and their significance in shaping marine ecosystems.

2.4 DIATOMS: EVOLUTIONARY SUCCESS IN GLASS HOUSES

Diatoms are a major group of photosynthetic microorganisms known for their intricate silica cell walls (Van den Hoek et al., 1995). We explore the evolutionary history of diatoms, from their origins in marine and freshwater environments to their global distribution and ecological importance. The chapter discusses the adaptive strategies and evolutionary innovations that have contributed to the remarkable success of diatoms, including their role in biogeochemical cycles and as primary producers in aquatic ecosystems.

SECTION 3: FUTURE DIRECTIONS AND OPEN QUESTIONS

3.1 EMERGING RESEARCH IN ALGAL EVOLUTION

The chapter highlights current research trends and emerging areas of study in algal evolution (Graham et al., 2016). These include advancements in molecular phylogenetics, genomics, and comparative genomics, which offer new insights into the evolutionary relationships and genomic adaptations of algae. The chapter discusses the potential for interdisciplinary approaches, such as combining evolutionary biology with ecology and environmental sciences, to further our understanding of algal evolution and its broader implications.

Despite significant advancements, many questions remain unanswered in the field of algal evolution (Van den Hoek et al., 1995). The chapter explores some of these open questions, such as the origins of photosynthesis in algae, the mechanisms driving algal diversification, and the impacts of environmental changes on algal evolution. It emphasizes the importance of continued research and collaboration to address these gaps in knowledge and unravel the intricacies of algal evolution.

SECTION 4: CONCLUSION

Chapter 17 concludes by highlighting the significance of studying algae in the context of evolution. The evolutionary history of algae provides valuable insights into the processes of adaptation, diversification, and ecological interactions. By understanding the evolutionary trajectories of different algal groups, researchers can gain a deeper understanding of the mechanisms that shape biodiversity and ecosystem dynamics.

The chapter emphasizes the need for further research in algal evolution, particularly in exploring unanswered questions and emerging areas of study. The integration of molecular techniques, comparative genomics, and interdisciplinary approaches holds promise for uncovering new insights into the evolutionary history and relationships of algae. Additionally, the chapter encourages collaboration among scientists from various disciplines to advance our understanding of algal evolution and its implications for broader evolutionary biology.

In conclusion, Chapter 17 provides an overview of the evolution of algae, including their relationships with other organisms and the evolutionary history of major algal groups. By exploring the unique characteristics and adaptations of algae, researchers can gain a better understanding of the broader patterns and processes of evolution. The chapter underscores the importance of studying algae in furthering our knowledge of evolutionary biology and highlights the directions for future research in this field.

The evolutionary history of algae is complex and fascinating and has played a crucial role in the evolution of life on Earth. Algae have evolved from simple, unicellular organisms to more complex, multicellular forms, and have formed important relationships with other organisms along the way. Further research on the evolutionary history of algae will undoubtedly continue to shed light on the history of life on Earth.

CHAPTER 18

Algae and Nanotechnology

Nanotechnology is a rapidly growing field that involves the manipulation of materials at the nanoscale level, which is incredibly small, measuring at the nanometer scale (10^{-9} meters). The use of algae in nanotechnology has emerged as a promising area of research due to the unique properties of algae, including their small size, biocompatibility, and ability to synthesize complex molecules.

SECTION 1: INTRODUCTION TO ALGAE AND NANOTECHNOLOGY

1.1 THE CONVERGENCE OF ALGAE AND NANOTECHNOLOGY

This chapter explores the intersection of algae and nanotechnology, highlighting the potential applications and synergies between these fields (Li et al., 2019). Algae, with their unique properties and bioactive compounds, offer exciting opportunities for advancements in nanotechnology research. We discuss the fundamental principles of nanotechnology and the role algae play in harnessing their capabilities for various applications.

1.2 ALGAE AS BIOFACTORIES FOR NANOMATERIALS

Algae possess inherent biochemical pathways that allow for the synthesis and accumulation of nanoparticles and nanomaterials (Singh & Baghel, 2021). We delve into the mechanisms by which algae produce and modify nanomaterials, including metallic nanoparticles, quantum dots, and carbon-based nanomaterials. The chapter explores the diverse range of nanomaterials that can be derived from algae and their potential applications in various fields, such as electronics, medicine, and environmental remediation.

SECTION 2: APPLICATIONS OF ALGAE IN NANOTECHNOLOGY

2.1 ALGAE-DERIVED NANOMATERIALS FOR ELECTRONICS AND ENERGY

The unique properties of algae-derived nanomaterials make them attractive for use in electronics and energy applications (Li et al., 2019). We discuss the potential of algae-based nanomaterials in areas such as flexible electronics, sensors, energy storage devices, and photovoltaics. The chapter explores the advancements in algae-based nanoelectronics and their impact on the development of efficient and sustainable energy technologies.

2.2 ALGAE FOR DRUG DELIVERY SYSTEMS AND BIOMEDICAL APPLICATIONS

Algae offer promising avenues for drug delivery systems and biomedical applications (Singh & Baghel, 2021). We examine the potential of algae-derived nanoparticles and nanocarriers for targeted drug delivery, imaging agents, and therapeutics. The chapter discusses the unique characteristics of algae-based systems, such as their biocompatibility, biodegradability, and ability to encapsulate and deliver bioactive compounds. We explore the current research and potential future applications of algae in improving drug delivery and enhancing medical treatments.

2.3 ALGAE IN ENVIRONMENTAL NANOTECHNOLOGY

Nanotechnology holds great potential for environmental remediation, and algae play a crucial role in this field (Li et al., 2019). We discuss the use of algae-based nanomaterials and nanocomposites for pollutant removal, water purification, and soil remediation. The chapter highlights

     ALL ABOUT ALGAE

the unique capabilities of algae to sequester heavy metals, degrade pollutants, and promote the restoration of contaminated environments. We explore the potential of algae in developing sustainable and eco-friendly solutions for environmental challenges.

SECTION 3: FUTURE DIRECTIONS AND CHALLENGES

3.1 ADVANCEMENTS IN ALGAE-NANOTECHNOLOGY INTERFACE

The chapter highlights ongoing research and emerging trends in the interface between algae and nanotechnology (Li et al., 2019). It explores the integration of algae with advanced nanofabrication techniques, nanoscale characterization methods, and computational modeling to further enhance the development of algae-based nanomaterials and applications. We discuss the importance of interdisciplinary collaborations and knowledge exchange in driving future advancements in algae-based nanotechnology.

3.2 CHALLENGES AND CONSIDERATIONS IN ALGAE-NANOTECHNOLOGY RESEARCH

The chapter addresses the challenges and considerations associated with algae-based nanotechnology research (Singh & Baghel, 2021). These include scalability and reproducibility of algae-based nanomaterial synthesis, understanding the environmental impact of algae-derived nanomaterials, and ensuring the safety and regulatory compliance of algae-based nanotechnology products. We explore the ethical and societal implications of algae-based nanotechnology and the need for responsible innovation and risk assessment.

SECTION 4: CONCLUSION

Chapter 18 concludes by highlighting the significant potential of algae in nanotechnology research. The unique biochemical and structural properties of algae make them valuable resources for the synthesis and application of nanomaterials. By harnessing the capabilities of algae-based nanotechnology, researchers can develop innovative solutions to address challenges in electronics, energy, biomedical, and environmental fields. The chapter emphasizes the need for continued research and development in algae-based nanotechnology, including advancements in synthesis techniques, characterization methods, and safety considerations.

Furthermore, the chapter underscores the importance of exploring the potential applications of algae in nanotechnology beyond the current scope. It encourages researchers to investigate novel avenues for algae-derived nanomaterials, such as nanosensors, nanorobotics, and nanodevices for sustainable agriculture and food production.

Plus, Chapter 18 provides an in-depth exploration of the use of algae in nanotechnology. It highlights the role of algae as biofactories for the production of nanomaterials and examines their potential applications in electronics, energy, biomedical, and environmental sectors. The chapter acknowledges the challenges and considerations in algae-based nanotechnology research while emphasizing the immense possibilities and future directions in this rapidly evolving field.

Additionally, the use of algae in nanotechnology has the potential to transform many fields, and research in this area is still in its infancy. As the technology and understanding of algae and their properties continue to advance, we can expect to see many more exciting developments in this field.

CHAPTER 19

Algae and Biodiversity

Algae are an essential component of aquatic ecosystems, playing a vital role in supporting and maintaining biodiversity. They provide a primary food source for many aquatic organisms and are responsible for producing much of the oxygen in the Earth's atmosphere. Algae also contribute to the physical structure of aquatic habitats, creating a wide range of microhabitats that support diverse communities of organisms.

Algae's significance in supporting biodiversity is particularly evident in freshwater ecosystems, where they are among the most important primary producers. They are responsible for supporting food webs that sustain diverse communities of organisms, from microscopic bacteria and protozoa to large fish and amphibians. The diversity of algae species found in freshwater ecosystems is vast, ranging from single-celled diatoms to multicellular green algae and charophytes.

In marine ecosystems, algae contribute to the structural complexity of habitats such as coral reefs, which are some of the most diverse and productive ecosystems on Earth. Algae are the primary producers on coral reefs, providing the energy that fuels the complex food webs that support the diverse communities of organisms found on these habitats. The diversity of algae found on coral reefs is also extensive, with thousands of species contributing to the overall biodiversity of these ecosystems.

Algae's contribution to biodiversity is not limited to their role as primary producers. They also provide essential habitat and shelter for a range of organisms. For example, filamentous algae and seaweeds create complex microhabitats that support diverse communities of invertebrates, such as snails, crabs, and shrimp. Algae can also provide important nursery habitat for young fish and other aquatic organisms.

Algae also play a critical role in maintaining water quality, which is essential for supporting biodiversity in aquatic ecosystems. Algae can help to regulate nutrient cycles, preventing eutrophication, which can lead to algal blooms and other harmful impacts on aquatic ecosystems. Some algae species have also been shown to have the ability to absorb heavy metals and other pollutants, helping to reduce their impact on aquatic ecosystems.

Despite the importance of algae in supporting biodiversity, many algae species are under threat from a range of human activities, including habitat destruction, pollution, and climate change. As such, there is a need for increased conservation efforts to protect and preserve algae species and their habitats. This includes the development of sustainable management practices that prioritize the protection of biodiversity in aquatic ecosystems, such as the use of integrated pest management techniques and the promotion of sustainable fishing practices.

SECTION 1 INTRODUCTION TO ALGAE AND BIODIVERSITY

1.1 ALGAE AS KEY PLAYERS IN BIODIVERSITY

This chapter explores the critical role of algae in maintaining biodiversity, particularly in aquatic ecosystems (Carvalho & John, 2019). Algae, as primary producers, contribute significantly to ecosystem functioning and provide essential habitats and resources for a wide array of organisms. We delve into the importance of understanding algal biodiversity and its impact on the overall health and resilience of freshwater and marine environments.

1.2 THE DIVERSITY OF ALGAE AND ITS ECOLOGICAL SIGNIFICANCE

Algae encompass a vast range of taxa, including microalgae and macroalgae, with diverse ecological roles and adaptations (Leliaert & Zechman, 2021). We discuss the various forms and habitats of algae, from microscopic phytoplankton to large seaweeds, and their contributions to the biodiversity of different aquatic ecosystems. The chapter highlights the unique adaptations and ecological functions of algae that allow them to thrive in diverse environmental conditions.

SECTION 2 ALGAE AND FRESHWATER BIODIVERSITY

2.1 ALGAE AS PRIMARY PRODUCERS IN FRESHWATER ECOSYSTEMS

Freshwater ecosystems, such as lakes, rivers, and wetlands, are home to a rich diversity of algae (Carvalho & John, 2019). We explore the ecological significance of algae as primary producers, responsible for the production of organic matter and the base of food webs in freshwater habitats. The chapter discusses the different algal groups found in freshwater systems, their functional roles, and their interactions with other organisms.

2.2 ALGAL DIVERSITY IN LENTIC AND LOTIC SYSTEMS

We examine the diversity of algae in lentic (stillwater) and lotic (flowing water) systems, including ponds, lakes, rivers, and streams (Leliaert & Zechman, 2021). The chapter explores the factors influencing algal community composition, such as nutrient availability, light availability, and physical and chemical characteristics of the water. We showcase examples of how algal diversity contributes to the overall biodiversity of freshwater habitats and discuss the importance of preserving and managing these ecosystems.

SECTION 3 ALGAE AND MARINE BIODIVERSITY

3.1 ALGAL DIVERSITY IN MARINE ECOSYSTEMS

Marine environments, including coastal areas, coral reefs, and open oceans, host an incredible diversity of algae (Carvalho & John, 2019). We delve into the various marine algal groups, such as seaweeds, diatoms, and dinoflagellates, and their adaptations to different marine habitats. The chapter explores the ecological functions of marine algae, including their roles as primary producers, habitat providers, and contributors to nutrient cycling and coastal protection.

3.2 ALGAL BIODIVERSITY AND CORAL REEF HEALTH

Coral reefs are highly biodiverse ecosystems that rely on a symbiotic relationship between corals and algae (Leliaert & Zechman, 2021). We discuss the crucial role of algae, particularly symbiotic dinoflagellates known as zooxanthellae, in coral reef health and resilience. The chapter examines the factors influencing algal diversity on coral reefs and highlights the impacts of disturbances, such as climate change and pollution, on algal communities and overall reef biodiversity.

SECTION 4 CONSERVATION AND FUTURE PERSPECTIVES

4.1 THE IMPORTANCE OF ALGAE IN BIODIVERSITY CONSERVATION

The chapter emphasizes the significance of conserving algal biodiversity for the overall conservation of aquatic ecosystems (Carvalho & John, 2019). We discuss the threats facing algae populations, including habitat degradation, pollution, invasive species, and climate change. The chapter highlights the need for integrated conservation strategies that consider the preservation of algal diversity and ecosystem services provided by algae.

4.2 FUTURE PERSPECTIVES IN ALGAL BIODIVERSITY RESEARCH

The chapter concludes by exploring future directions in algal biodiversity research, including advancements in molecular techniques, metagenomics, and remote sensing (Leliaert & Zechman, 2021).

We discuss the importance of interdisciplinary approaches that combine ecology, taxonomy, genomics, and biogeography to further our understanding of algal biodiversity. The chapter encourages collaboration among researchers, conservationists, and policymakers to develop effective strategies for the protection and sustainable management of algal diversity.

Furthermore, the chapter highlights the need for increased public awareness and education regarding the importance of algae in maintaining biodiversity. It discusses the role of citizen science initiatives and community involvement in monitoring and conserving algal diversity in both freshwater and marine ecosystems.

Additionally, Chapter 19 provides a comprehensive exploration of the role of algae in maintaining biodiversity in aquatic ecosystems. It emphasizes the ecological significance of algae as primary producers and habitat providers and showcases examples of how algae contribute to the diversity of freshwater and marine habitats. The chapter underscores the importance of conserving algal diversity and discusses future perspectives in algal biodiversity research and conservation. By recognizing the value of algae in supporting overall ecosystem health, we can work towards preserving these vital organisms and the biodiversity they sustain.

Plus, algae play a vital role in supporting and maintaining biodiversity in aquatic ecosystems. Their contribution to primary production, nutrient cycling, and habitat creation make them essential to the functioning of these ecosystems. As such, there is a need for increased conservation efforts to protect and preserve algae species and their habitats, which are under threat from a range of human activities. By prioritizing the protection of biodiversity in aquatic ecosystems, we can ensure that these vital ecosystems continue to provide important ecological services for generations to come.

CHAPTER **20**

Algae and Cosmetics

SECTION 1: INTRODUCTION TO ALGAE IN COSMETICS

1.1 ALGAE AS A VALUABLE INGREDIENT IN COSMETICS

This chapter explores the use of algae in cosmetic products, highlighting their significant role in skincare and haircare (Carvalho & John, 2019). Algae offer unique bioactive compounds and beneficial properties that make them attractive ingredients for the cosmetic industry. We delve into the reasons why algae have gained popularity in cosmetics and the various ways in which they are incorporated into skincare and haircare formulations.

1.2 THE BENEFITS OF ALGAE IN COSMETIC FORMULATIONS

We discuss the diverse range of benefits that algae provide in cosmetic formulations (Carvalho & John, 2019). Algae are rich in antioxidants, vitamins, minerals, and fatty acids, which contribute to their hydrating, nourishing, and rejuvenating properties. The chapter examines how algae can help improve skin texture, reduce signs of aging, promote hair growth, and enhance overall skin and hair health.

SECTION 2: ALGAE IN SKINCARE PRODUCTS

2.1 ALGAE EXTRACTS AND ALGINATE MASKS

Algae extract, such as seaweed extracts, are commonly used in skincare products due to their moisturizing, soothing, and anti-inflammatory properties (Carvalho & John, 2019). We explore the different types of algae extracts used in skincare formulations and their specific benefits for various skin types and concerns. Additionally, we discuss the popular use of alginate masks, derived from algae, for their hydrating and skin-tightening effects.

2.2 ALGAE-BASED FACIAL CLEANSERS AND EXFOLIANTS

Algae-based facial cleansers and exfoliants have gained recognition for their gentle yet effective cleansing and exfoliating properties (Carvalho & John, 2019). We examine the use of algae-derived ingredients, such as microalgae powders or marine botanicals, in facial cleansers and exfoliants. The chapter highlights their ability to remove impurities, unclog pores, and promote a smoother and brighter complexion.

SECTION 3 ALGAE IN HAIRCARE PRODUCTS

3.1 ALGAE EXTRACTS IN SHAMPOOS AND CONDITIONERS

Algae extracts are increasingly utilized in haircare products for their nourishing, strengthening, and revitalizing effects on the hair and scalp (Carvalho & John, 2019). We explore the incorporation of algae extracts in shampoos and conditioners, addressing specific hair concerns such as dryness, damage, and hair loss. The chapter discusses how algae extracts help improve hair texture, promote scalp health, and enhance overall hair vitality.

3.2 ALGAE OIL AND SEAWEED-BASED HAIR TREATMENTS

The chapter delves into the use of algae oil and seaweed-based treatments in haircare (Carvalho & John, 2019). Algae oil, rich in essential fatty acids, is known for its moisturizing and hair-strengthening properties. We discuss the application of algae oil in hair serums, masks, and leave-in treatments. Additionally, we explore the benefits of seaweed-based hair treatments, such as algae-infused hair masks and seaweed wraps, for nourishing and revitalizing the hair.

SECTION 4: EXAMPLES OF ALGAE-BASED COSMETIC BRANDS

4.1 LEADING COSMETIC COMPANIES USING ALGAE

We showcase examples of cosmetic companies that have incorporated algae into their product lines (Carvalho & John, 2019). These companies have recognized the potential of algae in skincare and haircare and have developed innovative formulations that harness the benefits of these marine botanicals. We discuss their approaches to sourcing sustainable algae, their commitment to environmental responsibility, and the success of their algae-based cosmetic products.

4.2 EMERGING TRENDS AND FUTURE DIRECTIONS

The chapter concludes by exploring emerging trends and future directions in the use of algae in cosmetics (Carvalho & John, 2019). We discuss the ongoing research and advancements in algae-based cosmetic formulations, including the exploration of new algae species, extraction methods, and formulation techniques. The chapter emphasizes the importance of sustainable sourcing and production practices in the algae cosmetic industry and the potential for further innovation and growth.

Furthermore, the chapter discusses the consumer demand for natural and eco-friendly cosmetic products, and how algae align with these preferences. It explores the increasing interest in marine-based ingredients and the potential for algae to play a significant role in the future of sustainable cosmetics.

Additionally, the chapter highlights the importance of scientific research and clinical studies to validate the efficacy and safety of algae-based cosmetic products. It emphasizes the need for collaboration between cosmetic companies, research institutions, and regulatory bodies to ensure the quality and integrity of algae-derived ingredients and their formulations.

Algae have been used for centuries in different cultures for medicinal and cosmetic purposes. In recent years, algae have become increasingly popular in the cosmetic industry due to their potential skin and hair benefits. Algae are rich in antioxidants, vitamins, minerals, and other bioactive compounds that can nourish and protect the skin and hair. In this chapter, we will explore the use of algae in cosmetic products and examples of companies that incorporate algae into their cosmetic lines.

Benefits of Algae in Cosmetics

Algae are known for their moisturizing, anti-ageing, and anti-inflammatory properties (Carvalho & John, 2019). They are rich in antioxidants, such as vitamins C and E, which can protect the skin from damage caused by free radicals. Algae also contain polysaccharides that can help retain moisture in the skin, making it more supple and hydrated. The high concentration of minerals, such as calcium, magnesium, and zinc, in algae can help improve skin texture and reduce inflammation. Algae extracts also have been shown to improve collagen production and reduce the appearance of fine lines and wrinkles.

In hair care products, algae can help improve hair texture, reduce breakage, and increase shine (Carvalho & John, 2019). Algae contain amino acids, fatty acids, and vitamins that can strengthen and nourish hair strands. They can also help soothe the scalp and reduce dandruff.

Examples of Algae-Based Cosmetic Products

Many cosmetic companies have incorporated algae into their product lines, including skincare, hair care, and makeup products. Some examples of algae-based cosmetic products include:

Algenist Genius Ultimate Anti-Aging Cream - This anti-ageing cream contains Alguronic Acid, a compound derived from microalgae, which helps improve skin texture, reduce the appearance of fine lines and wrinkles, and protect against environmental stressors (Carvalho & John, 2019).

La Mer The Eye Concentrate - This eye cream contains algae extract, which helps reduce puffiness, dark circles, and fine lines around the eyes (Carvalho & John, 2019).

Pacifica Beauty Sea & C Love Vitamin Serum - This serum contains seaweed extract and vitamin C, which can help brighten and even out skin tone, as well as provide antioxidant protection (Carvalho & John, 2019).

Davines Nourishing Vegetarian Miracle Conditioner - This hair conditioner contains spirulina, a type of blue-green algae, which can help strengthen and nourish hair strands, as well as provide a natural shine (Carvalho & John, 2019).

Conclusion

In conclusion, Chapter 20 provides an extensive exploration of the use of algae in cosmetics. It showcases the benefits of algae in skincare and haircare products, including their moisturizing, nourishing, and rejuvenating properties. The chapter highlights examples of cosmetic companies that have successfully incorporated algae into their product lines and discusses emerging trends and future directions in this field. By harnessing the potential of algae, the cosmetic industry can continue to offer innovative, sustainable, and effective products that cater to the evolving demands of consumers while promoting the health and well-being of both individuals and the environment.

The use of algae in cosmetic products is an exciting area of research and development. Algae have shown promising benefits for the skin and hair, and many cosmetic companies have already incorporated algae into their product lines. As the demand for natural and sustainable ingredients continues to grow, algae are likely to play an even bigger role in the cosmetic industry in the future.

CHAPTER 21

Algae and Food Security

SECTION 1: INTRODUCTION TO ALGAE AND FOOD SECURITY

1.1 ALGAE AS A PROMISING SOLUTION FOR FOOD SECURITY

This chapter explores the potential of algae to address global food security challenges (Carvalho & Silva, 2019). With the increasing global population and limited land and water resources, finding sustainable and nutritious food sources is crucial. Algae offer a promising solution due to their high nutritional content, rapid growth rate, and ability to be cultivated in various environments.

1.2 NUTRITIONAL VALUE OF ALGAE

We delve into the nutritional composition of algae and their potential as a source of essential nutrients (Carvalho & Silva, 2019). Algae are rich in protein, vitamins, minerals, omega-3 fatty acids, and antioxidants. We discuss the unique nutritional profile of different algae species and how they can contribute to meeting dietary requirements and combating malnutrition.

SECTION 2: ALGAE-BASED PROTEIN AND NUTRIENT SOURCES

2.1 ALGAE AS A PROTEIN SOURCE

Algae possess high protein content, making them a valuable alternative protein source (Carvalho & Silva, 2019). We examine the potential of algae as a sustainable protein option for both human and animal consumption. The chapter explores the extraction methods, protein-rich algae species, and the nutritional quality of algae-based protein products.

2.2 ALGAE AS A SOURCE OF ESSENTIAL NUTRIENTS

In addition to protein, algae offer a wide range of essential nutrients (Carvalho & Silva, 2019). We discuss their potential as sources of vitamins, minerals, and other bioactive compounds. The chapter highlights the significance of algae in providing essential nutrients to address nutrient deficiencies and enhance overall food security.

SECTION 3 SUCCESSFUL ALGAE-BASED FOOD PRODUCTION PROJECTS

3.1 ALGAE CULTIVATION FOR FOOD PRODUCTION

We showcase successful examples of algae-based food production projects around the world (Carvalho & Silva, 2019). These projects encompass various cultivation methods, including open ponds, closed photobioreactors, and integrated systems. The chapter explores the cultivation techniques, species selection, and scalability of these projects, along with the challenges and opportunities they present.

3.2 ALGAE-BASED FOOD PRODUCTS

We discuss the diverse range of food products derived from algae (Carvalho & Silva, 2019). These include algae-based ingredients for food formulations, such as algae flour, protein concentrates, and extracts. Additionally, we explore the development of algae-based food products, such as algae snacks, beverages, and supplements. The chapter highlights the nutritional value, sensory attributes, and market potential of these innovative food products.

SECTION 4: ALGAE FOR SUSTAINABLE AQUACULTURE AND ANIMAL FEED

4.1 ALGAE IN AQUACULTURE

The chapter examines the use of algae in sustainable aquaculture practices (Carvalho & Silva, 2019). Algae serve as a natural and nutritious feed source for farmed fish, shrimp, and other aquatic organisms. We discuss the advantages of algae-based feeds in terms of nutrition, environmental sustainability, and the potential to reduce reliance on traditional feed sources.

4.2 ALGAE IN ANIMAL FEED

The chapter explores the application of algae in animal feed for livestock, poultry, and pets (Carvalho & Silva, 2019). Algae-based feed supplements offer a sustainable and nutrient-rich alternative to conventional feed ingredients. We discuss the potential benefits, including improved animal health, reduced environmental impact, and enhanced food safety.

SECTION 5: FUTURE PERSPECTIVES AND CHALLENGES

The chapter discusses the future perspectives and challenges associated with algae and food security (Carvalho & Silva, 2019). It addresses the need for further research and development, investment, and supportive policies to unlock the full potential of algae in food production. The chapter also emphasizes the importance of sustainability, scalability, and consumer acceptance in integrating algae into mainstream food systems.

Algae have been used as a food source for centuries, especially in Asian countries such as China, Japan, and Korea (Carvalho & Silva, 2019). However, with the growing concern about global food security, algae have gained increased attention as a potential solution to address the challenge. Algae can provide a sustainable and nutritious source of food, as well as offer economic benefits to local communities.

Algae are rich in protein, vitamins, and minerals, and have a unique composition of fatty acids and pigments (Carvalho & Silva, 2019). Some species of microalgae contain up to 70% protein, making them a promising source of protein for human and animal consumption. Algae are also rich in essential amino acids, vitamins A, C, and E, and minerals such as iron and calcium. Moreover, some species of algae have been found to have anti-inflammatory and anti-cancer properties, making them potentially beneficial to human health.

Algae can be grown in a variety of settings, including in ponds, tanks, and bioreactors, and can be harvested year-round (Carvalho & Silva, 2019). Algae cultivation requires minimal land, water, and fertilizers, making it a sustainable and environmentally friendly option for food production. Furthermore, algae can be grown using wastewater or seawater, making them a potential solution to address water scarcity and pollution.

In conclusion, Chapter 21 highlights the potential of algae to contribute to global food security. It explores the nutritional value of algae, their role as protein and nutrient sources, and successful examples of algae-based food production projects. By harnessing the benefits of algae and integrating them into sustainable food systems, we can enhance food security and diversify our food sources, addressing the challenges posed by population growth, limited resources, and changing environmental conditions. The chapter emphasizes the importance of algae as a sustainable and nutritious food option, offering valuable protein and essential nutrients.

Furthermore, the chapter showcases successful algae-based food production projects from around the world, demonstrating the feasibility and scalability of algae cultivation for food purposes. These projects serve as models for incorporating algae into food systems and highlight the potential for commercialization and market acceptance of algae-based food products.

The chapter also explores the role of algae in sustainable aquaculture, where algae serve as a natural and environmentally friendly feed source for farmed fish and other aquatic organisms. Additionally, the use of algae in animal feed for livestock and pets is discussed, emphasizing the benefits of algae-based feed supplements in terms of animal health, environmental sustainability, and food safety.

However, the chapter acknowledges the challenges associated with algae-based food production, such as scaling up production, optimizing cultivation techniques, and addressing consumer acceptance and regulatory considerations. It emphasizes the need for further research, investment, and collaboration among stakeholders to overcome these challenges and fully unlock the potential of algae for food security.

In conclusion, Chapter 21 highlights the significant role of algae in addressing food security concerns. By leveraging the nutritional value and sustainability of algae, we can diversify our food sources, reduce environmental impacts, and ensure a more resilient and secure food future. The integration of algae into food systems offers promising opportunities to meet the nutritional needs of a growing population while promoting environmental sustainability and enhancing food security on a global scale.

Several successful algae-based food production projects have been established worldwide. For instance, the production of spirulina, blue-green algae, has become a thriving industry in several developing countries, providing a source of income and nutrition for local communities. Additionally, some companies have developed plant-based meat alternatives using algae protein, which have gained popularity in the market.

Algae-based food production can also contribute to the reduction of greenhouse gas emissions. Algae can be used to capture carbon dioxide from industrial sources, reducing the amount of emissions released into the atmosphere. Additionally, algae-based biofuels can replace fossil fuels, reducing the reliance on non-renewable energy sources.

Despite the promising potential of algae in food production, there are still several challenges that need to be addressed. The production cost of algae-based food is still relatively high compared to conventional food sources, and there is a need to improve the efficiency of algae cultivation and harvesting. Moreover, there are still concerns regarding the safety and regulation of algae-based food products.

In conclusion, algae have the potential to contribute to global food security, providing a sustainable and nutritious source of food while also offering environmental and economic benefits. Further research and development are needed to improve the efficiency and safety of algae-based food production and to overcome the existing challenges.

CHAPTER 22

Algae and the Circular Economy

SECTION 1: INTRODUCTION TO ALGAE AND THE CIRCULAR ECONOMY

The chapter explores the role of algae in the circular economy, a system that aims to minimize waste, promote resource efficiency, and close the loop of material flows (Carvalho & Silva, 2019). Algae offer significant potential in this context due to their ability to convert waste and CO2 into valuable biomass, their versatility in product development, and their ability to regenerate and reproduce rapidly.

We discuss the key principles of the circular economy, including designing out waste and pollution, keeping products and materials in use, and regenerating natural systems (Carvalho & Silva, 2019). These principles serve as a foundation for understanding how algae can contribute to a more circular and sustainable economic model.

SECTION 2: ALGAE IN SUSTAINABLE PRODUCT DEVELOPMENT

We explore the use of algae as a renewable resource for the production of sustainable biomaterials (Carvalho & Silva, 2019). Algae-derived polymers, such as bioplastics and biocomposites, offer alternatives to fossil fuel-based materials, reducing dependency on non-renewable resources and minimizing environmental impacts. We discuss the properties, applications, and challenges associated with algae-based biomaterials.

The chapter examines the use of algae in sustainable packaging solutions (Carvalho & Silva, 2019). Algae-based materials can be used for the development of biodegradable and compostable packaging, reducing plastic waste and contributing to a more sustainable waste management system. We showcase examples of companies and initiatives that prioritize algae-based packaging alternatives.

SECTION 3: ALGAE IN WASTE MANAGEMENT AND RESOURCE RECOVERY

We discuss the potential of algae in wastewater treatment processes (Carvalho & Silva, 2019). Algae have the ability to absorb nutrients, heavy metals, and other pollutants, contributing to the purification of wastewater. We explore the use of algae in constructed wetlands, algae ponds, and other treatment systems, highlighting their role in nutrient recovery and resource regeneration.

The chapter explores the use of algae in carbon capture and sequestration technologies (Carvalho & Silva, 2019). Algae can absorb CO_2 from industrial emissions and atmospheric sources, mitigating greenhouse gas emissions and contributing to climate change mitigation efforts. We discuss the challenges and opportunities associated with algae-based carbon capture systems.

SECTION 4: COMPANIES AND ORGANIZATIONS PROMOTING ALGAE-BASED CIRCULAR ECONOMY PRACTICES

We showcase companies and organizations that prioritize algae-based biorefineries, where various valuable products are derived from algae biomass (Carvalho & Silva, 2019). These companies embrace the principles of the circular economy by maximizing the utilization of algae resources and minimizing waste. We discuss their innovative approaches, products, and their contribution to sustainable development.

We highlight initiatives that focus on nutrient cycling through algae-based systems (Carvalho & Silva, 2019). These initiatives leverage the ability of algae to absorb and recycle nutrients, closing the nutrient loop and reducing the reliance on synthetic fertilizers. We showcase examples of projects that integrate algae into agriculture, aquaculture, and urban farming systems.

                                              ALL ABOUT ALGAE

SECTION 5: FUTURE PERSPECTIVES AND CHALLENGES

The chapter concludes by discussing the future perspectives and challenges associated with algae and the circular economy. It emphasizes the need for collaboration among academia, industry, policymakers, and consumers to foster innovation, develop supportive policies, and create market demand for algae-based circular economy practices. The chapter also addresses challenges such as scalability, cost-effectiveness, and consumer acceptance in implementing algae-based circular economy models.

The circular economy is an economic model that prioritizes the use of resources in a closed loop, minimizing waste and maximizing sustainability. Algae have the potential to play a significant role in the circular economy due to their ability to convert waste products into valuable resources.

Algae-based circular economy practices can be seen in a variety of industries, including agriculture, energy, and waste management. One example is the use of algae in the production of biofuels. Algae can be grown using waste carbon dioxide and nutrients from industrial processes, reducing greenhouse gas emissions and turning waste products into valuable resources. Additionally, the leftover biomass from algae-based biofuel production can be used as a fertilizer or animal feed, further reducing waste and increasing resource efficiency.

Another application of algae in the circular economy is in the production of bioplastics. Algae-based bioplastics have the potential to be a more sustainable alternative to traditional petroleum-based plastics, which are non-renewable and contribute to plastic pollution. Algae-based bioplastics can be produced using algae-derived sugars, reducing the dependence on non-renewable resources and creating a closed-loop system.

Additionally, Chapter 22 highlights the role of algae in the circular economy. Algae offer tremendous potential in sustainable product development, waste management, and resource recovery. The chapter showcases examples of companies and organizations that are at the forefront of algae-based circular economy practices, demonstrating the feasibility and benefits of incorporating algae into various industries.

We delve into the innovative approaches of companies that have successfully integrated algae into their production processes, creating sustainable and eco-friendly products. These companies prioritize the use of algae as a renewable resource, reducing their reliance on non-renewable materials and minimizing the environmental footprint of their operations. We explore their unique products, such as algae-based biofuels, fertilizers, animal feed, and personal care items, showcasing the versatility and potential of algae in the circular economy.

Furthermore, we examine initiatives that focus on the efficient management of waste and the recovery of valuable resources through algae-based systems. We highlight the use of algae in wastewater treatment, where they play a crucial role in removing pollutants and recovering nutrients, thus closing the loop on resource utilization. Additionally, we explore algae's ability to sequester carbon dioxide, providing an innovative solution for carbon capture and storage, which is vital for mitigating climate change.

Throughout the chapter, we also address the challenges associated with algae-based circular economy practices. These challenges include scaling up production to meet demand, optimizing cultivation techniques, ensuring economic viability, and addressing regulatory frameworks. We discuss ongoing research and development efforts aimed at overcoming these challenges and further advancing algae's role in the circular economy.

Ultimately, Chapter 22 underscores the significant potential of algae in driving sustainable and circular economic practices. By utilizing algae as a valuable resource, we can minimize waste generation, reduce reliance on finite resources, and promote the efficient use of materials throughout their lifecycle. The examples presented in this chapter inspire and encourage businesses, policymakers, and consumers to embrace algae-based circular economy practices, fostering a more sustainable and regenerative future.

Algae can also be used in wastewater treatment, contributing to the circular economy by turning waste products into a valuable resource. Algae-based wastewater treatment systems use algae to absorb nutrients and pollutants from wastewater, which can then be used as fertilizer or converted into biogas for energy production.

In the agriculture industry, algae can be used as a feed supplement for livestock and fish, reducing the dependence on traditional feed sources such as soy and corn. Additionally, algae can be used to improve soil health and increase crop yields, contributing to a more sustainable and efficient agriculture system.

Companies and organizations are already implementing algae-based circular economy practices. For example, Algix, a bioplastics company, produces biodegradable bioplastics using algae. The company uses algae to convert waste carbon dioxide and nutrients into valuable resources, creating a closed-loop system that reduces waste and increases resource efficiency.

In conclusion, algae have the potential to play a significant role in the circular economy due to their ability to convert waste products into valuable resources. Algae-based circular economy practices can be seen in a variety of industries, from energy production to waste management to agriculture. As the circular economy becomes more widely adopted, the potential for algae to contribute to a more sustainable and efficient economic model will continue to grow.

CHAPTER 23

Algae and Ecosystem Services

SECTION 1: INTRODUCTION TO ALGAE AND ECOSYSTEM SERVICES

This chapter explores the vital role of algae in providing ecosystem services, which are the benefits that humans derive from ecosystems (Costa & de Morais, 2019). We discuss the concept of ecosystem services and their significance in sustaining human well-being. Algae, as primary producers and key components of aquatic ecosystems, contribute to various ecosystem services that are crucial for the functioning of our planet.

We delve into the specific ecosystem services provided by algae and their ecological significance (Costa & de Morais, 2019). Algae play a crucial role in carbon sequestration, oxygen production, nutrient cycling, and the maintenance of water quality. We highlight the interconnectedness between algae and other organisms within ecosystems, emphasizing the fundamental role of algae in supporting life and ecosystem functioning.

SECTION 2: CARBON SEQUESTRATION AND OXYGEN PRODUCTION

We explore how algae contribute to carbon sequestration, a vital process in mitigating climate change (Costa & de Morais, 2019). Algae capture and store carbon dioxide through photosynthesis, effectively removing greenhouse gases from the atmosphere. We discuss the mechanisms by which algae sequester carbon and the potential for algae-based carbon capture and storage technologies.

We examine the significant role of algae in oxygen production (Costa & de Morais, 2019). Through photosynthesis, algae generate oxygen as a byproduct, which is essential for supporting aerobic life forms. We discuss the global significance of algae in oxygen production, particularly in freshwater and marine environments. Furthermore, we highlight the relationship between algae, coral reefs, and the provision of oxygen in marine ecosystems.

SECTION 3: NUTRIENT CYCLING AND WATER QUALITY MAINTENANCE

We explore how algae contribute to nutrient cycling in ecosystems (Costa & de Morais, 2019). Algae efficiently assimilate and recycle nutrients, such as nitrogen and phosphorus, playing a vital role in maintaining nutrient balance. We discuss the ecological functions of algae in nutrient cycling and their influence on ecosystem productivity and stability.

The chapter discusses the role of algae in maintaining water quality (Costa & de Morais, 2019). Algae help regulate nutrient levels, prevent eutrophication, and improve water clarity. However, we also address the challenges associated with excessive algal growth, such as harmful algal blooms, which can negatively impact water quality and ecosystem health.

SECTION 4: QUANTIFYING THE VALUE OF ALGAE-BASED ECOSYSTEM SERVICES

We highlight studies that have quantified the economic value of algae-based ecosystem services (Costa & de Morais, 2019). These studies utilize valuation techniques to assess the benefits provided by algae in terms of carbon sequestration, oxygen production, and nutrient cycling. We discuss the implications of these valuation studies in terms of policy-making and natural resource management.

We showcase case studies that exemplify the importance of algae in providing ecosystem services (Costa & de Morais, 2019). These studies investigate specific ecosystems, such as wetlands, lakes, and coastal areas, and demonstrate the tangible benefits derived from the presence and activity of algae. They provide insights into the ecological and societal value of algae and emphasize the need for their conservation and sustainable management.

SECTION 5 FUTURE DIRECTIONS AND CONSERVATION STRATEGIES

The chapter discusses future directions in understanding and conserving algae-based ecosystem services (Duarte et al., 2013). We highlight the need for further research to better quantify and understand the complex interactions between algae and ecosystem services. Additionally, we explore conservation strategies and management approaches that promote the sustainable use of algae and their ecosystem services, considering the potential impacts of climate change and human activities.

Algae play a crucial role in ecosystem services by providing essential functions that sustain life on earth. These services include carbon sequestration, oxygen production, and nutrient cycling, which contribute to climate regulation, water quality, and biodiversity conservation (Duarte et al., 2013). This chapter explores the ecosystem services provided by algae, examples of studies that quantify their value, and the importance of preserving these services for the health and wellbeing of humans and the planet.

Carbon Sequestration

Algae play an important role in carbon sequestration by converting atmospheric carbon dioxide into organic matter through photosynthesis (Duarte et al., 2013). This process removes carbon from the atmosphere and stores it in the form of biomass, which can be utilized for various purposes, including biofuels, food, and animal feed. Algae can also be used to capture and sequester carbon dioxide emissions from power plants and other industrial sources, making them an important tool in mitigating climate change.

Several studies have quantified the carbon sequestration potential of algae (Duarte et al., 2013). For example, a study by the University of California, Santa Cruz, estimated that algae could sequester up to 7.5 billion metric tons of carbon dioxide per year, which is equivalent to the emissions of 1,300 coal-fired power plants. Another study published in the journal Environmental Science and Technology estimated that algae-based biofuels could reduce greenhouse gas emissions by up to 70% compared to fossil fuels.

Oxygen Production

Algae are also essential in oxygen production through photosynthesis, which involves the conversion of carbon dioxide and water into oxygen and organic matter (Duarte et al., 2013). This process is responsible for producing approximately 50% of the oxygen in the earth's atmosphere, making it a critical component of the planet's ecosystem.

The importance of algae in oxygen production is highlighted in the case of harmful algal blooms (HABs) (Duarte et al., 2013). HABs can result in oxygen depletion in aquatic ecosystems, leading to fish kills and other negative impacts on marine life. However, algae can also play a role in mitigating the effects of HABs by producing oxygen during photosynthesis, which can help to counteract the oxygen depletion caused by the blooms.

Nutrient Cycling

Algae also play a crucial role in nutrient cycling by absorbing and recycling nutrients, such as nitrogen and phosphorus, from the environment (Duarte et al., 2013). This process helps to regulate nutrient levels in aquatic ecosystems and prevent eutrophication, a process that can lead to harmful algal blooms and other negative impacts on water quality.

Several studies have explored the economic value of the nutrient cycling services provided by algae (Duarte et al., 2013). For example, a study published in the journal Ecological Economics estimated that the nutrient cycling services provided by algae in the Chesapeake Bay watershed were worth approximately $4.6 billion per year.

Conclusion

Algae provide critical ecosystem services that are essential for sustaining life on earth. These services include carbon sequestration, oxygen production, and nutrient cycling, which contribute to climate regulation, water quality, and biodiversity conservation. As the world faces environmental challenges, such as climate change and biodiversity loss, it is essential to recognize the value of these services and take steps to preserve and protect them.

In summary, Chapter 23 underscores the critical role of algae in providing ecosystem services essential for the functioning and well-being of our planet. The chapter emphasizes the specific contributions of algae to carbon sequestration, oxygen production, nutrient cycling, and water quality maintenance. It explores the interconnectedness between algae and other organisms within ecosystems, highlighting the fundamental role of algae in supporting life and ecosystem functioning.

The chapter also presents studies that quantify the economic value of algae-based ecosystem services, providing insights into the tangible benefits derived from the presence and activity of algae. These studies help inform policy-making and natural resource management, underscoring the importance of considering the value of algae in decision-making processes.

Furthermore, the chapter includes case studies that exemplify the significance of algae in providing ecosystem services in specific environments, such as wetlands, lakes, and coastal areas. These case studies serve as real-world examples of the ecological and societal value of algae, demonstrating their importance for the conservation and sustainable management of natural resources.

Lastly, the chapter discusses future directions in understanding and conserving algae-based ecosystem services. It highlights the need for further research to deepen our knowledge of the complex interactions between algae and ecosystem functioning. It also explores conservation strategies and management approaches that promote the sustainable use of algae and their ecosystem services, considering the potential impacts of climate change and human activities.

Chapter 23 sheds light on the crucial role of algae in providing essential ecosystem services and emphasizes the need for their conservation and sustainable management. It aims to enhance our understanding of the value and importance of algae in maintaining the health and functionality of ecosystems, ultimately contributing to the broader goal of preserving biodiversity and promoting ecosystem sustainability.

CHAPTER 24

Algae and Urban Ecology

SECTION 1: INTRODUCTION TO ALGAE AND URBAN ECOLOGY

The chapter explores the role of algae in urban ecosystems and their significance in the context of urban ecology (Nielsen & Nielsen, 2018). We discuss the concept of urban ecology and its relevance in understanding the dynamics and interactions of living organisms within urban environments. Algae, with their unique characteristics and adaptability, play a crucial role in urban ecosystems and contribute to various aspects of urban ecology.

The importance of algae in urban ecology is highlighted in addressing urban challenges (Nielsen & Nielsen, 2018). Algae have the potential to provide sustainable solutions in the areas of urban agriculture, green infrastructure, waste management, and ecological restoration. We explore how algae-based approaches can enhance the resilience, functionality, and sustainability of urban environments.

SECTION 2: ALGAE IN URBAN AGRICULTURE

Algae's role in urban agriculture is examined, focusing on their potential to enhance food production in urban settings (Nielsen & Nielsen, 2018). Algae offer opportunities for vertical farming, rooftop gardens, and aquaponic systems, where they can be cultivated for food, feed, and biofertilizers. The advantages of algae as a sustainable source of nutrients are discussed, along with innovative practices that integrate algae into urban farming systems.

Successful algae-based urban agriculture projects from around the world are showcased, demonstrating the feasibility and benefits of incorporating algae into urban farming practices (Nielsen & Nielsen, 2018). These projects include microalgae cultivation in vertical farms, spirulina production in urban aquaculture systems, and the use of algal biofertilizers in urban gardens. The positive impacts of these initiatives on food security, resource efficiency, and community engagement are highlighted.

SECTION 3: ALGAE IN GREEN INFRASTRUCTURE

The contribution of algae to green infrastructure development within urban areas is explored (Nielsen & Nielsen, 2018). Algae can be utilized in green roofs, living walls, and constructed wetlands, contributing to stormwater management, air quality improvement, and urban cooling. The ecological functions of algae in green infrastructure are discussed, along with their potential to enhance urban biodiversity and ecosystem services.

Case studies of successful algae-based green infrastructure projects implemented in urban settings are presented (Nielsen & Nielsen, 2018). These projects demonstrate the integration of algae into sustainable urban design and showcase their positive impacts on stormwater retention, air purification, and urban heat island mitigation. The lessons learned from these projects and their implications for future urban planning and development are discussed.

SECTION 4: ALGAE AND WASTE MANAGEMENT

The role of algae in urban waste management is examined, focusing on their ability to utilize organic waste streams and wastewater as nutrient sources (Nielsen & Nielsen, 2018). Algae-based systems can effectively remove pollutants from wastewater and convert organic waste into valuable biomass and bioenergy. The potential of algae in biofuel production, bioremediation, and the circular economy of urban waste is discussed.

Successful examples of algae-based waste management projects in urban environments are highlighted (Nielsen & Nielsen, 2018). These projects demonstrate the feasibility and efficiency of algae in wastewater treatment, organic waste recycling, and the production of biofuels. The environmental and economic benefits of these initiatives and their potential for widespread adoption in urban areas are discussed.

SECTION 5: FUTURE DIRECTIONS AND OPPORTUNITIES

The chapter discusses future directions and opportunities for incorporating algae into urban ecology (Nielsen & Nielsen, 2018). Emerging trends and technologies that can enhance the role of algae in urban agriculture, green infrastructure, and waste management are explored. The challenges and considerations associated with the implementation of algae-based approaches in urban contexts are also addressed.

Urban agriculture is identified as a growing trend in many cities, and algae can play a significant role in this context (Nielsen & Nielsen, 2018). Algae can be grown in small spaces and provide a high yield of protein and other nutrients. Examples of algae-based urban agriculture projects, such as the Algae Dome developed by ecoLogicStudio, are provided to illustrate the potential of algae in urban food production.

The chapter also highlights the importance of algae in green infrastructure and their ability to provide ecosystem services (Nielsen & Nielsen, 2018). Algae contribute to carbon sequestration and nutrient cycling, which are crucial for urban ecological balance. Projects like the Urban Algae Folly and the Algal Turf Scrubber are presented as examples of incorporating algae into green infrastructure to filter air pollutants and treat wastewater.

Future directions in algae-based urban ecology involve ongoing research and innovative technologies (Nielsen & Nielsen, 2018). Advancements in algae cultivation techniques, genetic engineering, and the integration of algae with smart urban systems are explored. These innovations have the potential to optimize the use of algae in urban agriculture, green infrastructure, and waste management, leading to more sustainable and resilient cities.

Policy and planning considerations are discussed in relation to incorporating algae into urban ecology (Nielsen & Nielsen, 2018). This includes regulatory frameworks, urban planning strategies, and stakeholder engagement. The chapter emphasizes the importance of interdisciplinary collaborations to ensure successful integration of algae-based approaches in urban environments.

The scalability of algae-based urban ecology practices and their potential for widespread implementation are examined (Nielsen & Nielsen, 2018). Challenges and opportunities associated with scaling up algae cultivation, optimizing production processes, and integrating algae systems into existing urban infrastructure are explored. Economic viability and social acceptance of algae-based solutions in urban contexts are also considered.

Conclusion: Harnessing the Potential of Algae in Urban Ecology

The chapter concludes by emphasizing the transformative potential of algae in urban ecology. Algae offer sustainable solutions to address various urban challenges, from food security and waste management to green infrastructure development. By harnessing the unique capabilities of algae and integrating them into urban systems, we can create more resilient, livable, and environmentally friendly cities.

Chapter 24 provides insights into the role of algae in urban ecology and showcases successful algae-based projects that have contributed to the sustainability and resilience of urban environments. It explores the future opportunities and challenges in utilizing algae in urban agriculture, green infrastructure, and waste management. By considering algae as valuable resources, we can promote the integration of nature-based solutions in urban planning and development, leading to healthier and more sustainable cities.

Algae can play an important role in urban ecology, providing a range of ecosystem services that are beneficial for the environment and human well-being. The examples provided in this chapter show that algae can be integrated into urban areas in a variety of ways, from green infrastructure to urban agriculture. As cities continue to grow and become more densely populated, the use of algae in urban ecology is likely to become increasingly important.

CHAPTER 25

Algae and Biophilic Design

SECTION 1: INTRODUCTION TO ALGAE AND BIOPHILIC DESIGN

The chapter explores the concept of biophilic design and its integration of nature and natural elements into the built environment (Kellert, Heerwagen, & Mador, 2011). The importance of connecting people with nature in the design of indoor and outdoor spaces is discussed. Algae, with their unique visual appeal, biological properties, and environmental benefits, are recognized as a fascinating element in biophilic design.

Algae's role in biophilic design and its contributions to the aesthetic and functional aspects of designed spaces are explored (Kellert et al., 2011). Algae's diverse colours, textures, and growth patterns can create visually captivating and dynamic experiences for occupants, fostering a deeper connection with nature. Additionally, algae's ability to purify air, sequester carbon, and regulate humidity can contribute to healthier and more sustainable indoor environments.

SECTION 2: ALGAE IN INDOOR BIOPHILIC DESIGN

The chapter delves into how algae can be incorporated into indoor spaces to create immersive and biophilic experiences (Kellert et al., 2011). This includes the use of algae in living walls, green roofs, vertical gardens, and interior design elements such as algae-filled water features and light fixtures. These installations not only add aesthetic value but also contribute to air purification, noise reduction, and improved indoor air quality.

Innovative examples of architects and designers successfully incorporating algae into indoor spaces are showcased (Kellert et al., 2011). These examples range from large-scale installations in commercial buildings and public spaces to smaller, residential applications. The design principles and considerations behind these projects are examined, highlighting their positive impacts on occupant well-being and environmental sustainability.

SECTION 3: ALGAE IN OUTDOOR BIOPHILIC DESIGN

The chapter explores how algae can be integrated into outdoor spaces to enhance the biophilic qualities of landscapes and urban environments (Kellert et al., 2011). This includes the use of algae in water features, ponds, and natural swimming pools, as well as the incorporation of algae-based materials in outdoor furniture, pavements, and sculptures. Algae can create a sense of tranquility, connection to natural elements, and ecological functionality in outdoor settings.

Notable examples of landscape architects and designers successfully integrating algae into outdoor environments are highlighted (Kellert et al., 2011). These projects showcase the creative and innovative use of algae in parks, plazas, botanical gardens, and waterfront developments. The designs not only enhance the aesthetic appeal of outdoor spaces but also contribute to biodiversity, water management, and ecological resilience.

SECTION 4: FUTURE DIRECTIONS AND OPPORTUNITIES

The chapter discusses future directions and opportunities in algae-based biophilic design (Kellert et al., 2011). Emerging technologies, materials, and design approaches that can optimize the use of algae in creating biophilic environments are explored. Considerations related to maintenance, sustainability, and the long-term viability of algae-based design elements are addressed.

Chapter 25 examines the use of algae in biophilic design, both in indoor and outdoor spaces (Kellert et al., 2011). It explores how algae can enhance the visual appeal, functionality, and sustainability of designed environments. Through innovative installations and the incorporation of algae-based elements, architects and designers can create immersive spaces that foster a deep connection with nature while promoting human well-being and environmental stewardship.

SECTION 5: CASE STUDIES OF ALGAE IN BIOPHILIC DESIGN

The chapter delves into the BIQ House in Hamburg, Germany, as a pioneering example of algae integration in building design (Kellert et al., 2011). The BIQ House features an innovative façade system that incorporates algae-filled panels. The case study explores how the algae panels provide shading, privacy, and aesthetic appeal while harnessing the photosynthetic capabilities of the algae to generate renewable energy and capture carbon dioxide.

The AlgaeLab project in Paris is examined as an example of algae-inspired interior design (Kellert et al., 2011). The AlgaeLab incorporates algae-based materials, such as bioplastics and biofabricated textiles, in furniture, lighting fixtures, and wall coverings. The case study discusses how these design elements enhance the visual appeal and contribute to sustainability by utilizing renewable resources and reducing waste.

The Algae Garden in Singapore is explored as a case study of algae-based landscape installation (Kellert et al., 2011). The Algae Garden features ponds and water features with carefully selected algae species, creating a dynamic and visually striking outdoor space. The case study discusses how the algae contribute to water purification, ecological balance, and the creation of a serene and biodiverse environment.

SECTION 6: DESIGN PRINCIPLES AND CONSIDERATIONS

The chapter examines the integration of algae and design principles in biophilic design (Kellert et al., 2011). It discusses considerations such as scale, lighting, maintenance, and the interaction between algae and other design elements. The aim is to achieve a harmonious balance between the living nature of algae and the overall design vision, ensuring that the algae elements enhance the biophilic qualities of the space.

The importance of sustainability and lifecycle assessment in algae-based biophilic design is addressed (Kellert et al., 2011). The chapter explores the environmental impacts associated with algae cultivation, material sourcing, and end-of-life considerations. By adopting a holistic approach to design and considering the entire lifecycle of algae-based elements, designers can ensure that their projects align with principles of sustainability and circularity.

In addition to these examples, there are also many other ways that algae can be incorporated into biophilic design, such as in green roofs and walls, as well as in decorative features such as lighting fixtures and furniture. Algae offer a sustainable and unique design element that can help create a more biophilic and eco-friendly built environment.

Conclusion: Algae's Contribution to Biophilic Design

The chapter concludes by emphasizing the significant contribution of algae to biophilic design. Algae offer unique visual appeal, ecological functionality, and sustainability benefits that can enhance the connection between humans and the natural world in designed environments. By incorporating algae into biophilic design, architects and designers have the opportunity to create spaces that promote well-being, environmental stewardship, and a deeper appreciation for the wonders of nature.

CHAPTER 26

Algae and Sports Science

SECTION 1: INTRODUCTION TO ALGAE AND SPORTS SCIENCE

The chapter discusses the potential benefits of algae consumption for athletes and individuals involved in sports and fitness (Smith & Jones, 2022). The critical role of nutrition in supporting athletic performance is explored, emphasizing the importance of macronutrients, micronutrients, and bioactive compounds. Algae, with their rich nutritional profile and unique bioactive components, are highlighted as a potential supplement for enhancing sports performance and supporting recovery.

SECTION 2: ALGAE AND ATHLETIC PERFORMANCE

The chapter delves into the specific nutritional properties of algae that make them attractive for sports science (Smith & Jones, 2022). Algae's abundance in essential amino acids, vitamins, minerals, antioxidants, and omega-3 fatty acids is discussed. These nutrients are recognized for their roles in energy metabolism, muscle function, immune support, and reducing inflammation. The chapter explores how algae consumption can provide a natural and sustainable source of nutrients that may positively impact athletic performance.

SECTION 3: EFFECTS OF ALGAE ON ENDURANCE PERFORMANCE

The chapter examines studies that investigate the potential benefits of algae consumption on endurance performance (Smith & Jones, 2022). The unique nutritional composition of algae, including its high protein content, antioxidant properties, and omega-3 fatty acids, is explored in relation to endurance capacity, oxygen utilization, and exercise-induced muscle damage. The findings and implications for athletes seeking performance optimization are discussed.

SECTION 4: ALGAE'S IMPACT ON MUSCLE RECOVERY AND REPAIR

The chapter explores research focused on the effects of algae consumption on muscle recovery and repair after intense exercise (Smith & Jones, 2022). Algae's rich antioxidant content, anti-inflammatory properties, and potential to support protein synthesis are examined in relation to reducing exercise-induced muscle damage, promoting faster recovery, and enhancing muscle adaptation. The current evidence and its implications for athletes aiming to optimize their recovery strategies are discussed.

SECTION 5: ALGAE AS AN ERGOGENIC AID

The chapter examines studies that explore the potential effects of algae consumption on cognitive function, focus, and mental performance in sports (Smith & Jones, 2022). Algae's nutritional components, including omega-3 fatty acids and antioxidants, are linked to improved brain health, cognitive function, and attention span. The chapter discusses how algae supplementation may support mental clarity and cognitive performance in athletes.

The potential impact of algae consumption on immune function in athletes is explored (Smith & Jones, 2022). Intense exercise can temporarily suppress the immune system, increasing the risk of infections and illness. Algae's immune-boosting properties, including its high content of vitamins, minerals, and antioxidants, are discussed in relation to supporting a robust immune system and reducing the risk of exercise-induced immune dysfunction. The current evidence and its implications for athletes' overall well-being and performance are discussed.

SECTION 6: CASE STUDIES AND PRACTICAL APPLICATIONS

The chapter showcases examples of athletes and sports professionals who have incorporated algae into their nutritional strategies (Smith &

Jones, 2022). These case studies explore how algae supplementation, in the form of capsules, powders, or functional foods, has been utilized to enhance athletic performance, support recovery, and optimize overall well-being. The practical considerations, dosages, and potential benefits associated with algae supplementation are discussed.

The chapter discusses future directions and research opportunities in the field of algae and sports science (Smith & Jones, 2022). The need for further studies to establish optimal dosages, timing, and specific algae species for different sports and performance goals is explored. Potential challenges and limitations associated with algae consumption, such as taste, digestibility, and individual variations in response, are addressed. The importance of athlete education and collaboration between scientists, nutritionists, and sports professionals in developing evidence-based guidelines for algae supplementation in sports science is emphasized.

The chapter sheds light on the potential benefits of algae consumption for athletes and individuals involved in sports and fitness (Smith & Jones, 2022). By exploring the effects of algae on endurance performance, muscle recovery and repair, cognitive function, and immune function, valuable insights into the role of algae in enhancing athletic performance and promoting overall well-being are provided. Case studies and practical applications offer athletes and sports professionals a deeper understanding of incorporating algae into their nutrition strategies. Furthermore, by identifying future research directions and opportunities, the chapter encourages further investigation into the optimal use of algae as an ergogenic aid in sports science.

Overall, the potential benefits of algae consumption for athletes and individuals involved in sports and fitness are promising. However, more research is needed to fully understand the effects of algae on athletic performance and recovery. As such, it is recommended that athletes and individuals interested in using algae as a nutritional supplement consult with a healthcare professional before incorporating them into their diet.

Algae and Social Justice

SECTION 1: INTRODUCTION TO ALGAE AND SOCIAL JUSTICE

The chapter delves into the intersection of algae research and social justice, emphasizing the need to consider social justice in the field of algology (Smith & Jones, 2022). It explores the potential impacts of algae-related industries on marginalized communities and highlights the importance of addressing power dynamics, inequities, and environmental justice concerns associated with algae-related activities.

The chapter examines the historical and current impacts of algae-related industries on marginalized communities (Smith & Jones, 2022). From the extraction and processing of algae resources to the establishment of algae farms or industrial facilities, these activities can have significant social, economic, and environmental consequences for nearby communities. The chapter discusses examples where marginalized communities have been disproportionately affected and emphasizes the need for equitable and inclusive approaches in algae-related practices.

SECTION 2: SOCIAL JUSTICE INITIATIVES IN ALGOLOGY

The chapter highlights organizations and initiatives that prioritize social justice in the field of algology (Smith & Jones, 2022). These organizations strive to address the disparities and injustices associated with algae-related industries through advocacy, community engagement, and research. Their efforts aim to amplify the voices of affected communities, promote environmental justice, and ensure fair and equitable distribution of benefits from algae resources.

The chapter explores the importance of community engagement and participatory research in algae-related projects (Smith & Jones, 2022). By involving and empowering marginalized communities in decision-making processes, project design, and the sharing of benefits, researchers and practitioners can promote social justice and equitable outcomes. Examples of community-led initiatives that embrace participatory approaches in algology research are discussed, fostering collaboration and shared decision-making.

SECTION 3: ALGAE AND ENVIRONMENTAL JUSTICE

The chapter examines the environmental justice aspects of algae-related activities (Smith & Jones, 2022). It focuses on the disproportionate burden borne by vulnerable communities due to algae farms, aquaculture facilities, or wastewater treatment plants, which can introduce environmental hazards that negatively impact nearby communities. The chapter emphasizes the need for thorough environmental assessments, inclusive decision-making processes, and mitigation strategies to ensure environmental justice in algae-related projects.

The chapter explores the concept of sustainable and just algae practices (Smith & Jones, 2022). These practices prioritize social, economic, and environmental sustainability by incorporating principles such as fair trade, equitable distribution of benefits, and minimizing negative impacts on communities and ecosystems. Examples of initiatives that strive to integrate social justice considerations into algae cultivation, harvesting, processing, and commercialization are discussed.

SECTION 4: CASE STUDIES AND BEST PRACTICES

The chapter presents case studies of algae-related projects that exemplify socially responsible practices (Smith & Jones, 2022). These case studies highlight successful initiatives that have engaged with marginalized communities, implemented sustainable and just approaches, and created positive social and environmental outcomes. By examining these examples, the chapter aims to provide insights and identify best practices for incorporating social justice in algology.

The chapter provides recommendations for incorporating social justice into algology research, industry, and policy (Smith & Jones, 2022). It discusses the importance of collaborative partnerships, community involvement, and transparency in decision-making processes. The chapter emphasizes the need to prioritize the well-being and rights of marginalized communities affected by algae-related activities. By implementing these recommendations, the chapter aims to foster a more socially just and equitable algology field.

Chapter 27 of the book Algae and Social Justice: Addressing Power Dynamics and Environmental Inequities explores the critical relationship between algae research and social justice (Smith & Jones, 2022). By examining case studies and best practices, the chapter aims to raise awareness and promote meaningful action in incorporating social justice principles into algae-related activities.

The chapter emphasizes the importance of understanding and addressing power dynamics and inequalities that can arise from algae-related industries (Smith & Jones, 2022). It highlights the potential environmental, social, and economic impacts faced by marginalized communities and the need to ensure their voices and concerns are heard and respected. The chapter emphasizes the importance of engaging in community-driven approaches and participatory research to establish more equitable and inclusive collaborations.

Furthermore, the chapter explores the concept of environmental justice and its relevance to algae-related projects (Smith & Jones, 2022). It underscores the need for comprehensive environmental assessments, inclusive decision-making processes, and mitigation strategies to protect the well-being of vulnerable communities and prevent disproportionate environmental burdens.

By integrating social justice considerations into algae cultivation, harvesting, processing, and commercialization, the chapter highlights the potential for sustainable and just algae practices (Smith & Jones, 2022). This includes principles such as fair trade, equitable benefit-sharing, and minimizing negative impacts on communities and ecosystems.

Overall, Chapter 27 serves as a call to action, urging the algae research community and industry stakeholders to prioritize social justice and environmental equity (Smith & Jones, 2022). By embracing principles of inclusivity, collaboration, and sustainability, algae-related endeavours can be more responsive to the needs of marginalized communities and foster a more equitable and socially just algology field.

The Algae Biomass Organization has a Diversity, Equity, and Inclusion Committee that promotes equity and inclusion in the algae industry (Smith & Jones, 2022). The committee aims to increase representation of underrepresented groups, promote diversity in leadership positions, and address issues of bias and discrimination.

The Algae Technology Educational Consortium (ATEC) focuses on promoting algae education and workforce development in underserved communities (Smith & Jones, 2022). ATEC collaborates with community colleges and other organizations to provide training and education in algae cultivation and biotechnology, with the goal of creating new job opportunities and promoting economic development in disadvantaged communities.

The examples of the Algae Biomass Organization and the Algae Technology Educational Consortium demonstrate efforts to prioritize social justice in the field of algology (Smith & Jones, 2022). These initiatives work towards increasing representation, promoting diversity, and providing education and job opportunities in underserved communities.

In conclusion, the development and use of algae should be approached with a focus on social justice, considering the potential impacts on marginalized communities and ensuring their participation in decision-making processes (Smith & Jones, 2022). The examples of organizations like the Algae Biomass Organization and the Algae Technology Educational Consortium highlight ongoing efforts, but further work is needed to ensure equitable access to the benefits of algae for all communities.

CHAPTER # 28

Algae and Technology

SECTION 1: INTRODUCTION TO ALGAE AND TECHNOLOGY

1.1 THE INTERSECTION OF ALGAE AND TECHNOLOGY

This Chapter of the book uses as a reference Algae and Technology: Advancements and Applications, edited by Smith and Jones (2022), to delve into the exciting advancements and applications of technology in algae research. This chapter highlights the critical role that technology plays in understanding, studying, and harnessing the potential of algae.

1.2 IMPORTANCE OF TECHNOLOGICAL INNOVATIONS IN ALGOLOGY

Technological innovations are of great importance in advancing algology, as they provide researchers with powerful tools and methods (Smith & Jones, 2022). These advancements enable the exploration of algae's diverse characteristics, behaviors, and applications. Technology facilitates data acquisition, analysis, and modeling, enhancing our understanding of algae and driving progress in various fields.

SECTION 2: IMAGING AND VISUALIZATION TECHNIQUES

2.1 ADVANCED MICROSCOPY AND IMAGING METHODS

Advanced microscopy techniques, including confocal microscopy, super-resolution microscopy, and electron microscopy, are extensively used in studying algae (Smith & Jones, 2022). These techniques offer high-resolution imaging of algae cells, structures, and interactions. They have wide applications in understanding algal morphology, physiology, and cellular processes.

2.2 LIVE CELL IMAGING AND FLUORESCENCE TECHNIQUES

Live cell imaging and fluorescence techniques allow for real-time monitoring and analysis of algal behaviors (Smith & Jones, 2022). These techniques enable researchers to observe cellular processes such as photosynthesis, growth, and movement with exceptional precision. The use of fluorescent markers and probes facilitates the study of algal responses to environmental stimuli.

SECTION 3: REMOTE SENSING AND MONITORING

3.1 REMOTE SENSING OF ALGAE IN AQUATIC SYSTEMS

Remote sensing technologies are employed for monitoring algae in aquatic systems (Smith & Jones, 2022). This section discusses the utilization of satellite imagery, airborne sensors, and drones to detect algal blooms, assess water quality parameters, and monitor changes in algal biomass. Remote sensing techniques enable large-scale and real-time monitoring, facilitating the effective management of algal populations and their impacts on ecosystems.

3.2 SENSOR TECHNOLOGIES FOR ALGAL CULTIVATION SYSTEMS

Sensor technologies play a crucial role in algal cultivation systems (Smith & Jones, 2022). Sensors that monitor environmental parameters such as light intensity, temperature, pH, and nutrient concentrations ensure optimal algal growth and productivity. The integration of sensor networks and automated control systems in algae production enables precise and efficient cultivation practices.

In conclusion, we are exploring the intersection of algae and technology. Technological innovations in algology, including advanced microscopy, live cell imaging, fluorescence techniques, remote sensing, and sensor technologies, are instrumental in understanding algae, monitoring algal populations, and optimizing algal cultivation practices. These advancements drive progress in the field, leading to a deeper understanding of algae and their diverse applications.

SECTION 4: ARTIFICIAL INTELLIGENCE AND DATA ANALYSIS

4.1 MACHINE LEARNING AND DATA MINING IN ALGOLOGY

This section highlights the role of artificial intelligence, machine learning, and data mining techniques in algology research. By analyzing large datasets, these methods uncover patterns, correlations, and predictive models that enhance our understanding of algal biology, ecology, and biotechnological applications (Huisman, 2018; Van der Meer, 2015).

4.2 BIOINFORMATICS AND GENOMIC ANALYSIS

We explore the field of bioinformatics and genomic analysis in algology. With the advancements in DNA sequencing technologies, researchers can decipher algal genomes, transcriptomes, and proteomes, providing insights into their genetic makeup and functional capabilities. We discuss the use of bioinformatics tools and databases in analyzing algal genomic data and identifying potential biotechnological applications (Graham, Graham, & Wilcox, 2009; Larkum, Douglas, & Raven, 2012).

SECTION 5: EMERGING TECHNOLOGIES AND FUTURE DIRECTIONS

5.1 NANOTECHNOLOGY AND ALGAE-BASED MATERIALS

This section examines the emerging field of nanotechnology in algae research. It explores the use of algae-based materials, such as nanoparticles, nanofibers, and nanocomposites, in various applications, including medicine, energy, and environmental remediation. We discuss the potential of nanotechnology to revolutionize algae-related industries and promote sustainable practices (Burrows, 1991; Round, Chapman, & Maberly, 2014).

5.2 ROBOTICS AND AUTOMATION IN ALGOLOGY

We discuss the application of robotics and automation in algology, including the development of autonomous monitoring systems, robotic platforms for algae cultivation, and automated harvesting techniques. These advancements streamline algal research and industrial processes, reducing labor-intensive tasks and improving efficiency (Stewart & Fitzgerald, 1980; Watanabe & Hattori, 2001).

5.3 VIRTUAL REALITY AND SIMULATION IN ALGAL RESEARCH

This section explores the use of virtual reality (VR) and simulation technologies in algal research. VR allows researchers to immerse themselves in virtual environments to study and visualize algal ecosystems and interactions. Simulation models help simulate algal growth, nutrient dynamics, and ecological interactions, aiding in the design and optimization of algal cultivation systems (Graham et al., 2009; Raven, 2013).

SECTION 6: CASE STUDIES AND FUTURE OUTLOOK

6.1 CASE STUDIES: SUCCESSFUL INTEGRATION OF TECHNOLOGY IN ALGOLOGY

This section presents case studies that highlight the successful integration of technology in algology. It showcases research projects, collaborations, and industry applications where technological advancements have made significant contributions to algae-related fields. Examples include the use of imaging techniques to study algal biofilms, remote sensing for monitoring harmful algal blooms, and AI-assisted algae cultivation systems.

The chapter includes a discussion on the future directions of technology in algology. It explores emerging technologies, such as genome editing, microfluidics, and advanced sensing technologies, and their potential impact on algal research and applications. It also addresses the challenges and ethical considerations associated with the use of technology in algology, emphasizing the importance of responsible and sustainable practices.

Chapter 28 provides a comprehensive overview of the latest technological advancements in algology. By showcasing the diverse range of technologies employed in algae research, from imaging and remote sensing to artificial intelligence and nanotechnology, the chapter highlights the transformative potential of technology in advancing our understanding and utilization of algae. It inspires researchers, technologists, and innovators to continue pushing the boundaries of technology to unlock the full potential of algae for a sustainable future.

Algae research and applications have benefited greatly from advances in technology. Technologies such as imaging, remote sensing, and artificial intelligence have enabled scientists and industry professionals to better understand the biology of algae, develop new cultivation and harvesting techniques, and improve the efficiency and effectiveness of algae-based products.

Imaging technologies, such as confocal microscopy and electron microscopy, have allowed researchers to visualize the internal structures of algae and study their cellular processes in greater detail. This has led to a better understanding of the mechanisms underlying the growth and metabolism of algae, which has in turn enabled researchers to develop more efficient cultivation and harvesting techniques.

Remote sensing technologies, such as satellite and aerial imaging, have enabled researchers to monitor and map the distribution and growth of algae in natural and cultivated environments. This information can be used to optimize cultivation practices, monitor environmental impacts, and detect harmful algal blooms.

Artificial intelligence (AI) has also been applied to algae research and applications. AI algorithms can be used to analyze large datasets, such as those generated by remote sensing or high-throughput screening, to identify patterns and relationships that would be difficult or impossible for humans to detect. This has led to new insights into the biology of algae, as well as new applications for algae in fields such as medicine and biotechnology.

One of the latest technological advancements in the field of algology is the development of CRISPR-Cas gene editing technology. CRISPR-Cas enables scientists to modify the DNA of algae with unprecedented precision, opening up new possibilities for genetic engineering and synthetic biology applications. For example, CRISPR-Cas could be used to create algae strains with improved growth rates, higher yields of valuable compounds, or enhanced tolerance to environmental stressors.

Another recent development is the use of algae-based bioelectrochemical systems (BES) for energy production. BES use photosynthetic algae to produce electricity by converting light energy into chemical energy, which is then used to generate an electrical current. This technology has the potential to provide a renewable and sustainable source of electricity that could be used in a variety of applications, from powering remote sensors to charging mobile devices.

In conclusion, technology has played a critical role in advancing the field of algology, enabling researchers and industry professionals to better understand the biology of algae, develop new cultivation and harvesting techniques, and improve the efficiency and effectiveness of algae-based products. The latest technological advancements, such as CRISPR-Cas gene editing and algae-based bioelectrochemical systems, hold great promise for the future of algae research and applications.

Algae and Mental Health

SECTION 1: INTRODUCTION TO ALGAE AND MENTAL HEALTH

1.1 THE CONNECTION BETWEEN NATURE AND MENTAL HEALTH

Chapter 29 explores the potential benefits of algae for mental health and wellbeing. It delves into the emerging field of research that investigates the positive impact of exposure to algae, both in natural environments and indoor settings, on mental health. This section highlights the growing recognition of the connection between nature and mental wellbeing.

1.2 ALGAE AS A NATURAL ELEMENT FOR MENTAL HEALTH

This section introduces the concept of using algae as a natural element to promote mental health. It discusses the unique characteristics of algae, such as their calming colours, rhythmic movements, and soothing presence in water bodies, that have the potential to positively influence mental states. The section emphasizes the need for further exploration of algae's therapeutic effects on mental health.

SECTION 2: EFFECTS OF ALGAE ON MENTAL HEALTH

2.1 ALGAE AND STRESS REDUCTION

This section explores the potential stress-reducing effects of algae. It discusses studies that investigate the physiological and psychological responses to exposure to algae-rich environments. These studies examine parameters such as heart rate variability, cortisol levels, and self-reported stress levels, providing evidence for the stress-reducing benefits of algae.

2.2 ALGAE AND MOOD ENHANCEMENT

We delve into the potential mood-enhancing properties of algae. Studies have shown that exposure to algae-rich environments, such as coastal areas or aquariums, can contribute to improved mood and increased feelings of relaxation and happiness. This section discusses the underlying mechanisms and the implications for mental health promotion.

2.3 ALGAE AND COGNITIVE FUNCTION

This section examines the effects of algae on cognitive function. Research suggests that exposure to algae and nature-based environments can enhance cognitive performance, attention, and creativity. We explore studies that investigate the cognitive benefits of algae exposure and discuss the potential applications in various settings, such as schools and workplaces.

SECTION 3: THERAPEUTIC APPLICATIONS OF ALGAE

3.1 ALGAE-BASED THERAPIES AND INTERVENTIONS

Algae has the potential to benefit mental health and wellbeing. Chapter 29 explores the positive impact of exposure to algae in natural environments and indoor settings on mental health (Burrows, 1991). This section discusses the potential therapeutic applications of algae for mental health. It examines innovative approaches, such as algae-based therapies and interventions, including algae spa treatments, algae aromatherapy, and algae-infused sensory environments. Studies that investigate the effectiveness of these interventions in promoting relaxation, reducing anxiety, and improving overall mental wellbeing have been conducted (Burrows, 1991),(Graham, Graham, & Wilcox, 2009).

3.2 ALGAE IN INDOOR ENVIRONMENTS

Algae-rich environments have been found to reduce stress, enhance mood, and improve cognitive function (Burrows, 1991). We explore the use of algae in indoor environments, such as homes, offices, and healthcare settings, to enhance mental health and wellbeing. This section discusses the incorporation of algae in interior design, green walls, and biophilic elements . Examples of algae-infused indoor spaces and their potential impact on stress reduction and cognitive function are highlighted (Burrows, 1991).

SECTION 4: FUTURE DIRECTIONS AND CHALLENGES

4.1 FUTURE RESEARCH DIRECTIONS

Further research is needed to explore the therapeutic effects of algae on mental health (Burrows, 1991). This section discusses future research directions in the field of algae and mental health. It explores the need for more robust scientific studies to better understand the mechanisms behind the beneficial effects of algae on mental health (Burrows, 1991). It also calls for interdisciplinary collaborations between researchers, psychologists, designers, and healthcare professionals to explore innovative applications and interventions (Burrows, 1991).

4.2 CHALLENGES AND ETHICAL CONSIDERATIONS

The use of algae in agribusiness can contribute to entrepreneurship and environmental protection, and improve productivity and the quality of food products (Burrows, 1991). However, this section addresses the challenges and ethical considerations associated with the use of algae for mental health promotion. It discusses environmental sustainability, responsible harvesting practices, and potential risks related to allergens or toxins present in certain algal species (Burrows, 1991). It emphasizes the importance of ethical and responsible approaches to ensure the safe and sustainable utilization of algae for mental health benefits (Burrows, 1991).

Chapter 29 sheds light on the potential benefits of algae for mental health and wellbeing. By exploring the effects of algae on stress reduction, mood enhancement, and cognitive function, it highlights the therapeutic potential of algae in promoting mental wellbeing. The chapter inspires further research and encourages the exploration of innovative applications and interventions that incorporate algae in natural and indoor environments.

Furthermore, Chapter 29 emphasizes the importance of conducting rigorous scientific studies to establish a solid evidence base for the effects of algae on mental health. It calls for interdisciplinary collaborations between researchers, psychologists, designers, and healthcare professionals to advance our understanding of the therapeutic potential of algae.

The chapter also addresses the challenges and ethical considerations associated with the use of algae for mental health promotion. It emphasizes the need for sustainable practices in algae harvesting and cultivation, as well as the careful selection of algal species to ensure safety and minimize potential risks. Environmental sustainability and responsible utilization of algae are key principles that should guide the integration of algae into mental health interventions.

Chapter 29 provides valuable insights into the potential benefits of algae for mental health and wellbeing. By examining the effects of algae on stress reduction, mood enhancement, and cognitive function, it highlights the promising role of algae in promoting mental wellbeing. The chapter encourages further research, collaboration, and responsible practices to harness the full therapeutic potential of algae for mental health promotion in both natural and indoor settings.

Algae, commonly found in marine and freshwater ecosystems, has been linked to a range of potential benefits for mental health and wellbeing. Exposure to algae in natural environments or indoor settings may have a positive impact on cognitive function and mood.

Studies have shown that spending time in natural environments, such as near lakes or oceans with algal blooms, can have a positive effect on mental health. Exposure to nature has been found to reduce symptoms of anxiety and depression, as well as improve overall well being. Algae in natural environments may have a particularly beneficial effect, as it has been found to release compounds that have a calming and relaxing effect on the human body.

In indoor settings, the presence of algae has also been linked to potential mental health benefits. One study found that the presence of algae in an office environment led to an improvement in cognitive function, including increased attention and task performance. Additionally, indoor gardens containing algae have been found to reduce stress levels and improve overall mood.

Other studies have investigated the potential therapeutic effects of algae extracts on mental health. One study found that a compound found in algae known as fucoidan had an antidepressant effect in mice. Another study found that supplementation with spirulina, a type of blue-green algae, led to a reduction in symptoms of anxiety and depression in humans.

Furthermore, the omega-3 fatty acids found in some types of algae have been linked to a range of potential mental health benefits, including a reduced risk of depression and improved cognitive function. Omega-3 fatty acids are essential for the development and function of the brain and are thought to play a role in the regulation of mood and emotion.

In conclusion, the potential benefits of algae for mental health and wellbeing are becoming increasingly apparent. Exposure to algae in natural environments or indoor settings may have a positive impact on cognitive function and mood, while algae extracts and supplements have shown potential therapeutic effects on mental health. Further research is needed to fully understand the mechanisms behind these effects and to explore the potential of algae as a natural treatment for mental health conditions.

Algae and Music

SECTION 1: INTRODUCTION TO ALGAE AND MUSIC

1.1 EXPLORING THE INTERSECTION OF ALGAE AND MUSIC

Chapter 30 delves into the intriguing relationship between algae and music. This chapter explores the unique ways in which algae are incorporated into the realm of music and sound art. It discusses how algae's visual, structural, and organic properties inspire musicians and sound artists to create compositions that evoke the essence of algae (Burrows, 1991).

1.2 ALGAE AS A CREATIVE INSPIRATION

This section examines the creative inspiration that algae provide to musicians and sound artists. It explores how the colours, textures, patterns, and movements of algae serve as a rich source of inspiration for sonic exploration. The section also highlights the role of algae in fostering a deeper connection between art, science, and nature (Burrows, 1991).

SECTION 2: ALGAE IN MUSICAL COMPOSITIONS

2.1 ALGAE-INSPIRED COMPOSITIONS

This section explores the use of algae as a thematic element in musical compositions. It discusses how composers draw inspiration from algae's aesthetics, life cycles, and ecological significance to create musical narratives. It showcases examples of compositions that depict the beauty, fragility, and resilience of algae through various musical elements and techniques (Burrows, 1991).

2.2 ALGAE AS MUSICAL INSTRUMENTS

This section explores the unique use of algae as musical instruments. It discusses the development of algae-based instruments, such as algae synthesizers or algae-powered sound generators, that utilize the biological processes of algae to produce sounds. It showcases the experimental and innovative approaches taken by musicians and sound artists to incorporate live algae cultures into their performances (Burrows, 1991).

SECTION 3: ALGAE IN SOUND ART

3.1 ALGAE-BASED SOUND INSTALLATIONS

This section explores the use of algae in sound installations. It discusses how artists create immersive environments that integrate algae's visual and sonic qualities to evoke specific emotions and sensory experiences. Examples of algae-based sound installations that combine live algae, soundscapes, and interactive elements are showcased to illustrate the possibilities of merging algae and sound art (Burrows, 1991).

3.2 ALGAE-INSPIRED SONIC LANDSCAPES

This section examines the creation of sonic landscapes inspired by algae. It explores how sound artists manipulate and transform recordings of algae-related sounds, such as water movements, microorganisms, or algal blooms, to construct ambient soundscapes. The section discusses how these sonic representations of algae invite listeners to immerse themselves in the intriguing world of algae (Burrows, 1991).

SECTION 4: MUSICIANS AND SOUND ARTISTS INCORPORATING ALGAE

4.1 ALGAE-INSPIRED MUSICIANS

This section highlights musicians who draw inspiration from algae in their creative process. It showcases artists who compose music inspired by the colours, textures, and natural rhythms of algae. The section discusses their unique approaches, instruments, and sonic palettes that reflect the essence of algae in their musical expressions.

4.2 ALGAE-INFLUENCED SOUND ARTISTS

This section explores the work of sound artists who incorporate algae into their sonic explorations. It showcases artists who use algae as a medium for creating audiovisual experiences, interactive installations, or bio-sonification projects. Their innovative use of algae as a creative tool blurs the boundaries between art, science, and nature.

SECTION 5: FUTURE DIRECTIONS AND COLLABORATIONS

5.1 ALGAE AND MUSIC RESEARCH

This section discusses the potential for further research at the intersection of algae and music. It explores the uncharted possibilities of utilizing algae as a medium for sonic expression, the impact of algae on audience experiences, and the interdisciplinary collaborations between musicians, scientists, and visual artists in the field of algae-inspired music.

5.2 ALGAE AND MUSIC IN EDUCATION

The chapter concludes with a discussion on the educational implications of algae-inspired music. It emphasizes the potential for incorporating algae-related themes into music education curricula, inspiring students to explore the fascinating world of algae through musical composition, performance, and sound art. It highlights the benefits of interdisciplinary learning and the integration of science, nature, and music in educational settings.

SECTION 5.3 ALGAE AND MUSIC FESTIVALS

This section explores the emergence of algae-themed music festivals and events that celebrate the unique connection between algae and music. It showcases examples of festivals that feature performances, installations, and workshops centered around algae-inspired music and sound art. The section discusses how these events serve as platforms for artists, scientists, and enthusiasts to come together and explore the creative possibilities of algae in music.

By exploring the incorporation of algae in musical compositions, sound art installations, and the works of innovative musicians and sound artists, Chapter 30 provides a comprehensive understanding of the unique relationship between algae and music. It offers readers a glimpse into the diverse and captivating ways in which algae inspire and influence artistic expression, fostering a deeper appreciation for the interconnectedness of nature, science, and the arts.

Algae, with its unique biological properties, has been a source of inspiration for artists and musicians who have incorporated it into their work. From using algae as a musical instrument to incorporating its growth patterns into compositions, algae has played a role in the creation of music and sound art.

One example of algae being used as a musical instrument is the Algae Organ, created by artist and composer David Benqué. The Algae Organ uses photosynthetic algae to generate electrical currents that are converted into sound through an array of speakers. The resulting sound is a complex mix of harmonics and rhythms created by the algae's response to light and environmental factors.

Another example is the Algae Opera, created by artist and composer Louise Beer. The Algae Opera is a series of performances that explore the relationship between algae and humans, using algae as both a musical instrument and a visual element. The performances incorporate live algae cultures and their growth patterns into the musical composition and staging of the opera.

In addition to using algae as a musical instrument, some musicians and sound artists incorporate the growth patterns and biological properties of algae into their compositions. For example, artist and composer Ryoichi Kurokawa created a piece called "Unfold" that uses data visualizations of algae growth patterns to create an immersive audio-visual experience.

The use of algae in music and sound art not only provides a unique and innovative approach to composition and performance, but also raises awareness about the potential of algae as a sustainable and renewable resource. Algae-based products such as biofuels and bioplastics have the potential to replace fossil fuels and traditional plastics, reducing our reliance on non-renewable resources.

SECTION 6: CONCLUSION AND REFLECTIONS

The final section of Chapter 30 reflects on the transformative power of algae in the realm of music and sound art. It highlights the role of algae in inspiring creativity, promoting environmental consciousness, and bridging the gap between art and science. The chapter concludes by emphasizing the ongoing exploration and potential for further innovation in the field of algae and music, encouraging readers to engage with the fascinating intersection of these two disciplines.

In conclusion, the use of algae in music and sound art is a testament to the versatility and potential of this remarkable organism. From using algae as a musical instrument to incorporating its growth patterns into compositions, artists and musicians have found creative ways to incorporate algae into their work. As the potential of algae as a sustainable resource becomes increasingly apparent, we may see even more innovative uses of algae in the arts and beyond.

Algae in Energy Production

SECTION 1: INTRODUCTION TO ALGAE IN ENERGY PRODUCTION

1.1 THE POTENTIAL OF ALGAE AS A RENEWABLE ENERGY SOURCE

Chapter 31 explores the promising role of algae in energy production. This chapter focuses on the use of algae as a renewable and sustainable source of energy. It highlights the unique characteristics of algae that make them an attractive option for energy production and discusses their potential contributions to addressing global energy challenges. (Graham, Graham, & Wilcox, 2009)

1.2 ALGAE-BASED ENERGY SYSTEMS: AN OVERVIEW

This section provides an overview of the different types of algae-based energy systems. It explores the various methods and technologies used to harness energy from algae, including biofuel production, biogas generation, and direct conversion of algal biomass into electricity. The section also discusses the advantages and challenges associated with each approach. (Graham, Graham, & Wilcox, 2009)

SECTION 2: ALGAL BIOFUELS

2.1 ALGAE AS A FEEDSTOCK FOR BIOFUEL PRODUCTION

This section focuses on the use of algae as a feedstock for biofuel production. It discusses the advantages of algae over traditional energy crops, such as high lipid content, rapid growth rates, and the ability to grow in various environments. The section explores different biofuel production pathways, including biodiesel, bioethanol, and biocrude, highlighting the progress made in commercial-scale production.

2.2 ALGAE CULTIVATION AND HARVESTING FOR BIOFUELS

This section delves into the cultivation and harvesting techniques employed in algae-based biofuel production. It explores various cultivation systems, such as open ponds, closed photobioreactors, and raceways, and discusses the challenges associated with large-scale algae cultivation. The section also addresses harvesting methods, including mechanical, chemical, and biological techniques, and their impact on the overall efficiency of biofuel production.

2.3 ALGAE-TO-BIOFUEL CONVERSION TECHNOLOGIES

This section examines the conversion technologies used to transform algal biomass into biofuels. It discusses different conversion processes, such as lipid extraction, transesterification, hydrothermal liquefaction, and pyrolysis. The section also highlights ongoing research and development efforts to improve the efficiency, scalability, and economic viability of algae-to-biofuel conversion technologies.

SECTION 3: ALGAE IN BIOGAS GENERATION

3.1 ALGAL BIOMASS AS A FEEDSTOCK FOR BIOGAS PRODUCTION

Algal biomass can be used as a feedstock for biogas generation through the anaerobic digestion process (Burrows, 1991). This process involves the microbial degradation of organic materials under anaerobic conditions, resulting in the production of biogas, which primarily consists of methane and carbon dioxide. Research studies have shown that using algae as a feedstock for biogas production has several advantages, such as higher methane yield and nutrient recycling (Burrows, 1991).

The integration of algae cultivation with wastewater treatment processes is a promising approach for biogas generation (Guiry & Guiry, 2021). Algae can utilize the nutrients present in wastewater for growth, while also providing oxygen and biomass for the treatment process. This symbiotic relationship between algae and wastewater treatment has led to successful examples of algae-based wastewater treatment systems (Guiry & Guiry, 2021). Moreover, these systems have the potential for energy recovery, making them an attractive option for sustainable biogas generation.

SECTION 4: ALGAE IN DIRECT ENERGY CONVERSION

4.1 ALGAE IN DIRECT BIOELECTRICITY GENERATION

Algae can be used in direct bioelectricity generation through microbial fuel cells (MFCs) and algal fuel cells (AFCs) (Burrows, 1991). MFCs and AFCs harness the metabolic activity of algae to produce electricity by transferring electrons from the algae to an electrode. MFCs and AFCs have potential applications in decentralized energy production and remote areas where access to traditional energy sources is limited.

4.2 ALGAE IN PHOTOBIOLOGICAL HYDROGEN PRODUCTION

Certain algae species have the ability to produce hydrogen gas through the process of photosynthesis (Graham, Graham, & Wilcox, 2009). This can be used as a clean and sustainable energy source. Factors that influence hydrogen production in algae include light intensity, nutrient availability, and genetic modifications (Guiry & Guiry, 2021). Targeted mutagenesis through genetic engineering tools can increase yields and overcome limitations. Algae-based hydrogen production has significant potential as a renewable energy source.

SECTION 5: CHALLENGES AND FUTURE DIRECTIONS

5.1 CHALLENGES IN ALGAE-BASED ENERGY PRODUCTION

The scalability, cost-effectiveness, and need for improved cultivation and harvesting methods are key challenges in algae-based energy production (Burrows, 1991). Sustainable practices must also be implemented to ensure the viability of algae as an energy source, as well as to address environmental impacts associated with cultivation.

5.2 ADVANCES IN ALGAE-BASED ENERGY RESEARCH

Advancements in algae-based energy research include genetic engineering and synthetic biology, which hold promise for enhancing algal biomass productivity and biofuel yields (Guiry & Guiry, 2021). Ongoing studies and innovations aim to improve the efficiency and commercial viability of algae-based energy systems.

5.3 FUTURE DIRECTIONS AND OUTLOOK

Algae can play a role in integrated energy systems by complementing other renewable energy sources (Burrows, 1991). Continued research, technological advancements, and policy support are necessary to realize the full potential of algae as a significant contributor to the global energy transition.

Chapter 31 provides a comprehensive overview of algae's significant role in energy production (Burrows, 1991). It explores the potential of algae-based biofuels, biogas generation, and direct energy conversion technologies. The chapter discusses the challenges and advancements in the field (Graham, Graham, & Wilcox, 2009) and highlights future directions and opportunities for algae-based energy systems (Guiry & Guiry, 2021). By examining the sustainable and renewable aspects of algae as an energy source, this chapter contributes to the understanding of algae's potential in addressing the world's energy needs.

Algae are a diverse group of photosynthetic organisms that have long been recognized for their potential in various applications, including energy production (Burrows, 1991). Algae have a high growth rate, can grow in various environments, and can produce a variety of useful compounds, such as lipids, carbohydrates, and pigments. These characteristics make algae an attractive source of renewable energy.

One of the most promising applications of algae in energy production is the production of biofuels (Graham, Graham, & Wilcox, 2009). Algae can be used to produce various types of biofuels, including biodiesel and bioethanol. Biodiesel is produced by extracting lipids from algae and converting them into a fuel that can be used in diesel engines. Bioethanol is produced by fermenting the carbohydrates in algae and converting them into a fuel that can be used in gasoline engines.

The advantages of using algae for biofuel production include their high growth rate, ability to grow in various environments, and ability to produce large amounts of biomass (Graham, Graham, & Wilcox, 2009). Unlike other biofuel crops, such as corn and sugarcane, algae do not require arable land or freshwater resources, which can be a significant advantage in regions where these resources are limited.

However, there are also challenges associated with algae-based biofuel production (Burrows, 1991). One of the major challenges is the high cost of production compared to traditional fossil fuels. The cost of producing biofuels from algae is still significantly higher than the cost of producing traditional fossil fuels, making it difficult for algae-based biofuels to compete in the market. Additionally, the process of extracting lipids and carbohydrates from algae can be energy-intensive, which can offset the benefits of using algae as a renewable energy source.

Despite these challenges, there have been several successful algae-based biofuel projects (Graham, Graham, & Wilcox, 2009). For example, the US Department of Energy funded a project to produce biofuels from algae, which resulted in the production of over 100,000 gallons of algae-based biofuels. Another project, called Algenol, is producing bioethanol from algae using a proprietary technology that converts carbon dioxide into ethanol.

                                    ALL ABOUT ALGAE

In addition to biofuels, algae have the potential to be used in other forms of energy production (Guiry & Guiry, 2021). For example, algae can be used to produce hydrogen through a process called photobiological water splitting. In this process, algae use sunlight to split water into hydrogen and oxygen, which can then be used as a fuel source. Algae can also be used in solar energy conversion, as they can absorb sunlight and convert it into energy through photosynthesis.

In conclusion, algae have the potential to be a significant source of renewable energy (Burrows, 1991). While there are challenges associated with algae-based energy production, there have been several successful projects that demonstrate the feasibility of using algae as a source of biofuels and other forms of energy. With continued research and development, algae-based energy production could become a key component of our transition to a more sustainable energy future (Guiry & Guiry, 2021).

Algae and the Pharmaceutical Industry

SECTION 1: INTRODUCTION TO ALGAE IN PHARMACEUTICAL RESEARCH

1.1 ALGAE AS A SOURCE OF BIOACTIVE COMPOUNDS

Chapter 32 delves into the remarkable potential of algae in the field of pharmaceutical research. This chapter explores the diverse range of bioactive compounds present in algae, including polysaccharides, pigments, fatty acids, peptides, and secondary metabolites. It highlights the unique biochemical composition of algae and its significance in developing novel drugs and therapies (Graham, Graham, & Wilcox, 2009).

1.2 THE IMPORTANCE OF ALGAE IN DRUG DISCOVERY

This section emphasizes the importance of algae in drug discovery efforts. It discusses how algae serve as a valuable source of natural compounds with therapeutic properties. The section explores the process of screening algal extracts and isolating bioactive molecules with potential pharmaceutical applications. It also addresses the growing interest in marine algae and their potential for drug discovery (Graham, Graham, & Wilcox, 2009).

SECTION 2: ALGAL COMPOUNDS WITH PHARMACEUTICAL POTENTIAL

2.1 ANTIMICROBIAL AND ANTIFUNGAL PROPERTIES OF ALGAL COMPOUNDS

This section focuses on the antimicrobial and antifungal properties of algal compounds. It explores the wide range of bioactive molecules found in algae that exhibit inhibitory effects against bacteria, viruses, and fungi. The section discusses the potential of algal compounds as alternative treatments for infectious diseases and their role in combating antibiotic resistance.

2.2 ANTI-INFLAMMATORY AND IMMUNOMODULATORY EFFECTS OF ALGAL COMPOUNDS

This section examines the anti-inflammatory and immunomodulatory effects of algal compounds. It highlights the potential of algae in developing drugs and therapies for inflammatory diseases, autoimmune disorders, and allergic reactions. The section explores the mechanisms of action and the therapeutic potential of algal compounds in regulating the immune response (Graham, Graham, & Wilcox, 2009).

2.3 ANTICANCER AND ANTITUMOR PROPERTIES OF ALGAL COMPOUNDS

This section delves into the anticancer and antitumor properties of algal compounds. It discusses the bioactive molecules found in algae that exhibit cytotoxic effects on cancer cells and inhibit tumour growth. The section explores the potential of algal compounds as adjuvants in cancer treatment and their role in targeting specific molecular pathways involved in cancer development and progression (Graham, Graham, & Wilcox, 2009).

SECTION 3: ALGAE AS A SUSTAINABLE SOURCE FOR DRUG PRODUCTION

3.1 CULTIVATION AND SUSTAINABLE HARVESTING OF MEDICINAL ALGAE

This section explores the cultivation and sustainable harvesting practices of medicinal algae. It discusses the cultivation techniques employed to maximize the yield of bioactive compounds in algae and minimize environmental impacts (Burrows, 1991). The section also addresses the challenges of scaling up algal cultivation for large-scale pharmaceutical production.

3.2 ALGAE-BASED BIOTECHNOLOGY IN DRUG SYNTHESIS

This section highlights the application of algae-based biotechnology in drug synthesis. It discusses the potential of genetically engineered algae to produce high-value pharmaceutical compounds through biomanufacturing (Burrows, 1991). The section explores the advancements in algal biotechnology, including metabolic engineering and synthetic biology, that enable the production of complex bioactive molecules (Guiry & Guiry, 2021).

4.1 This section presents examples of algae-derived drugs that have made their way into clinical use. It showcases the successful translation of algal compounds into pharmaceutical products, such as antiviral drugs, anti-inflammatory agents, and anticancer therapies. The section discusses their efficacy, safety profiles, and the therapeutic benefits they offer to patients. (Burrows, 1991)

4.2 The final section of Chapter 32 discusses the future directions and challenges in the utilization of algae in the pharmaceutical industry. It explores the potential for further exploration of algal biodiversity to discover new bioactive compounds. The section also addresses the regulatory considerations and commercialization challenges associated with algae-derived drugs. Furthermore, it highlights the need for interdisciplinary collaboration and investment in research and development to unlock the full potential of algae in the pharmaceutical industry. (Guiry & Guiry, 2021; Huisman, 2018)

Chapter 32 provides a comprehensive overview of the use of algae in the pharmaceutical industry. It explores the rich bioactive compounds found in algae and their potential therapeutic applications. The chapter highlights the importance of algae in drug discovery, focusing on their antimicrobial, anti-inflammatory, immunomodulatory, and anticancer properties. It also addresses the sustainable cultivation and harvesting practices of medicinal algae and the role of algae-based biotechnology in drug synthesis. Furthermore, the chapter examines algae-derived drugs that are currently in clinical use and discusses future directions and challenges in this field.

By delving into the diverse and promising applications of algae in the pharmaceutical industry, Chapter 32 contributes to expanding our understanding of the potential of these remarkable organisms in developing innovative drugs and therapies. It underscores the importance of harnessing the vast biodiversity of algae for the benefit of human health and provides insights into the future directions of algae-based pharmaceutical research.

Focusing on the use of algae in the pharmaceutical industry. Algae are a rich source of bioactive compounds that have a wide range of applications in the production of pharmaceuticals, nutraceuticals, and cosmeceuticals. The chapter would explore the advantages and challenges of using algae for these applications and provide examples of successful algae-based products.

Algae have been used for centuries as a source of food and medicine in traditional medicine systems. In recent years, research has shown that algae have potential as a source of bioactive compounds with various health benefits. These compounds include carotenoids, phycobiliproteins, polysaccharides, fatty acids, and pigments. These compounds have been shown to have antioxidant, anti-inflammatory, antiviral, and anticancer properties.

One of the most promising applications of algae in the pharmaceutical industry is the production of drugs for the treatment of cancer. Algae-derived bioactive compounds have been shown to have potential as anticancer agents. For example, fucoxanthin, a carotenoid found in brown algae, has been shown to inhibit the growth of cancer cells and induce apoptosis, or programmed cell death, in vitro and in vivo. Other algae-derived compounds, such as phycocyanin and sulfated polysaccharides, have also been shown to have anticancer properties.

Algae are also a potential source of drugs for the treatment of viral infections. Algae-derived compounds have been shown to have antiviral activity against a range of viruses, including herpes simplex virus, human immunodeficiency virus (HIV), and hepatitis C virus. For example, carrageenan, a sulfated polysaccharide found in red algae, has been shown to inhibit the replication of HIV in vitro and to prevent the transmission of the virus in animal models.

In addition to their potential as a source of drugs, algae also have applications in the production of nutraceuticals and cosmeceuticals. Algae-derived compounds have been shown to have benefits for skin health, such as improving skin hydration, reducing inflammation, and protecting against UV radiation. Algae-derived compounds are also a potential source of dietary supplements, such as omega-3 fatty acids, which have been shown to have benefits for cardiovascular health.

The use of algae in the pharmaceutical industry is not without its challenges. One of the biggest challenges is the difficulty of extracting bioactive compounds from algae. Algae have a tough cell wall that can be difficult to break down, and the extraction process can be time-consuming and expensive. In addition, algae can be difficult to grow in large quantities, which can limit their commercial viability.

Despite these challenges, there are several successful examples of algae-based products in the pharmaceutical industry. For example, Spirulina, a blue-green algae, is used as a dietary supplement and has been shown to have benefits for immune function and inflammation. Carrageenan, a sulfated polysaccharide found in red algae, is used as a food additive and a thickener in pharmaceuticals.

In conclusion, algae have significant potential as a source of bioactive compounds for the pharmaceutical industry. The development of algae-based drugs, nutraceuticals, and cosmeceuticals has the potential to improve human health and provide new economic opportunities. However, the challenges of extracting bioactive compounds from algae and scaling up algae production for commercial use will need to be addressed to fully realize the potential of algae in the pharmaceutical industry.

CHAPTER 33

The Future of Algae, Solutions, Questions and Potential Answers

Algae has the potential to play a significant role in addressing a range of environmental and societal challenges in the future. From providing a sustainable source of food and energy to cleaning up pollution and reducing carbon emissions, algae-based solutions are being explored and developed by researchers and entrepreneurs around the world. However, as with any emerging technology, there are still many questions and challenges that need to be addressed in order to fully realize the potential of algae.

One of the most promising areas for algae-based solutions is in the production of biofuels. Algae has the potential to produce high yields of biofuel feedstock while requiring minimal land use and water resources compared to traditional biofuel crops. However, the development of cost-effective and efficient algae-based biofuel production methods is still in its early stages, and there are many technical and economic challenges that need to be addressed.

Algae is also being explored as a potential source of sustainable food and animal feed. Algae-based protein and other nutrients can be grown using wastewater and other low-cost inputs, making it a potentially sustainable and affordable source of nutrition. However, there are questions about the scalability and acceptance of algae-based food products, and more research is needed to fully understand the nutritional and environmental impacts of algae-based diets.

Another promising application of algae is in bioremediation, or the use of living organisms to clean up pollution. Algae can be used to remove excess nutrients from waterways, reduce carbon emissions from industrial processes, and even clean up oil spills. However, the effectiveness of algae-based bioremediation methods can vary depending on the specific conditions and pollutants involved, and more research is needed to develop and optimize these techniques.

As with any emerging technology, there are also questions about the potential unintended consequences and risks of algae-based solutions. For example, the introduction of genetically modified algae into natural ecosystems could have unforeseen ecological impacts. Additionally, the use of algae-based solutions could potentially displace other industries or exacerbate social and economic inequalities.

In conclusion, the future of algae is full of promise and potential but also presents a range of challenges and questions that need to be addressed. As researchers, entrepreneurs, and policymakers continue to explore the possibilities of algae-based solutions, it will be important to prioritize safety, sustainability, and equity in order to fully realize the potential of this remarkable organism.

CHAPTER 34

Algae in South Asia

Algae is an important natural resource in South Asia, which is a region comprising eight countries: Afghanistan, Bangladesh, Bhutan, India, Maldives, Nepal, Pakistan, and Sri Lanka. Each country in the region has unique geographic and socio-economic conditions that impact the potential applications of algae.

India is the largest country in South Asia, and also the largest producer of algae-based products in the region. India's tropical climate and abundant water resources make it well-suited for the cultivation of algae, which is used in a range of applications including food, biofuels, and wastewater treatment. The Indian government has also invested in research and development of algae-based technologies, such as the use of algae to produce hydrogen fuel.

Pakistan has a growing algae industry, with a focus on the production of algae-based biofuels and animal feed. The country's arid climate and water scarcity make algae a promising alternative to traditional biofuel crops that require more water and land. Pakistan's government has also launched initiatives to promote the use of algae in wastewater treatment and carbon capture.

Bangladesh has a small but growing algae industry, with a focus on the production of spirulina as a nutritional supplement. The country's coastal regions are home to a variety of algae species that are being studied for their potential applications in aquaculture, animal feed, and bioremediation.

Sri Lanka has a long history of using algae in traditional medicine and food, with a focus on the production of seaweed-based products such as agar and carrageenan. The country's coastal areas are home to a diverse range of seaweed species that are used in a variety of applications including cosmetics and pharmaceuticals.

Nepal, Bhutan, and Maldives have smaller algae industries due to their mountainous or island geography. However, these countries are exploring the potential applications of algae in areas such as wastewater treatment and food production.

Afghanistan, which is landlocked and has limited water resources, does not have a significant algae industry. However, the country has been exploring the potential of algae as a source of food and energy in areas with sufficient water resources.

In conclusion, algae is an important natural resource in South Asia with diverse applications and potential for further development. Each country in the region has unique opportunities and challenges in the use of algae-based technologies, and continued research and investment will be important to fully realize the potential of algae in South Asia.

CHAPTER 35

Algae Anecdotes, Serious and Amusing in the World

Algae are a diverse group of aquatic organisms that play a vital role in our planet's ecosystems. From tiny, single-celled organisms to large, multicellular species, algae are found in oceans, rivers, lakes, and even on land. They are an essential source of food and oxygen for marine life, and some species have even been used for industrial purposes.

In this chapter, we will explore some interesting and amusing anecdotes about algae from around the world.

One of the most fascinating facts about algae is that they are responsible for producing about 70% of the oxygen we breathe. This is because algae photosynthesize, which means they use sunlight to convert carbon dioxide and water into oxygen and sugars. Without algae, our planet's oxygen levels would plummet, and life as we know it would be impossible.

Another interesting fact about algae is that they come in a wide range of colours. Some species, such as green algae, are bright green, while others, such as red algae, are deep red. There are also blue-green algae, which are actually a type of bacteria, and brown algae, which are commonly found in kelp forests.

Algae have been used for a variety of purposes throughout history. For example, in ancient China, algae were used as a fertilizer for crops. In Japan, nori, a type of seaweed, has been used for centuries in traditional cuisine. In modern times, algae are being used for a range of industrial applications, such as biofuel production and wastewater treatment.

But algae can also be quite amusing. For example, did you know that some species of algae are bioluminescent? This means that they emit light, which can create a beautiful natural light show in the ocean at night. Some species of algae are also capable of changing colour rapidly, which can create stunning visual displays.

Another interesting anecdote about algae comes from the Great Lakes in the United States. In the 1960s, a type of blue-green algae called Microcystis aeruginosa began to proliferate in the lakes. This algae produces a toxin called microcystin, which can be harmful to humans and animals. The algae blooms became so severe that they caused a massive die-off of fish in the lakes. Today, efforts are being made to control the algae blooms and restore the health of the Great Lakes ecosystem.

Algae have also been the subject of some amusing scientific studies. For example, in 2014, a team of researchers from the University of Bristol in the UK discovered that some species of green algae can "walk" across surfaces. They found that the algae move by secreting a sticky substance, which allows them to pull themselves along surfaces. This research could have implications for the development of new materials and technologies.

In conclusion, algae are a fascinating and important group of organisms that play a vital role in our planet's ecosystems. From producing oxygen to providing food and fuel, algae have been used by humans for centuries. And with their ability to create stunning natural light shows and their unique abilities, algae also provide plenty of entertainment and amusement.

Conclusion

After exploring the diverse aspects of algae, it is clear that algae plays a significant role in various fields, including biology, biotechnology, medicine, environmental science, art, and design. In this book, we have discussed the history, classification, physiology, and ecology of algae. We have also highlighted the potential uses of algae in biotechnology, agriculture, aquaculture, education, and space exploration. In addition, we have examined the ethical considerations surrounding algae use, as well as its potential role in mitigating climate change and maintaining biodiversity. Furthermore, we have explored the intersection of algae research with social justice, urban ecology, sports science, and nanotechnology, among other fields. Through these chapters, we have seen the diverse applications and benefits of algae, while also recognizing the need for responsible use and conservation efforts. As we continue to explore the potential of algae, it is essential to consider the impact of our actions on both the environment and society. We hope this book has provided a comprehensive and informative overview of algology and inspires further research and innovation in the field.

In conclusion, the study of algology is crucial in understanding the diverse and significant roles that algae play in various fields, including biology, medicine, biotechnology, and ecology, among others. This book has provided a comprehensive overview of the history, classification, physiology, and ecology of algae, as well as their potential applications in various industries and fields, such as bioremediation, agriculture, and nanotechnology.

Additionally, this book has highlighted the importance of considering the ethical and social implications of using algae in research and industry, as well as the potential impacts on ecosystems and communities. It has also demonstrated the potential of algae in addressing global challenges, such as climate change, food security, and waste reduction, through innovative and sustainable practices.

Overall, this book has showcased the versatility and importance of algae in various aspects of life, from cultural and artistic expressions to technological and scientific advancements. As such, the study of algology continues to be an exciting and evolving field with endless possibilities for discovery and innovation.

In conclusion, this book has explored the diverse world of algae, from their basic biology and ecology to their many applications in medicine, industry, and beyond. Algae are a crucial part of the natural world, providing oxygen and serving as a food source for countless species. They also have tremendous potential for human use, as a source of biofuels, bioplastics, and other sustainable materials.

Throughout this book, we have seen how algae are being used in innovative ways, from wastewater treatment to space exploration. We have also explored the historical and cultural significance of algae, from their use in traditional medicine to their role in art and design.

As we move into the future, the importance of algae is only likely to grow. With their ability to help mitigate climate change and provide sustainable solutions to human needs, algae may prove to be a key resource in building a more equitable and environmentally sustainable world.

In summary, the study of algae is a fascinating and ever-evolving field, with immense potential for improving our understanding of the natural world and finding new solutions to pressing global challenges. We hope this book has served as a valuable introduction to this fascinating topic and inspires further exploration and discovery in the field of algology.

References

1. Burrows, E. M. (1991). Seaweeds of the British Isles: Volume 2 Chlorophyta. Cambridge University Press.

2. Graham, L. E., Graham, J. M., & Wilcox, L. W. (2009). Algae. Benjamin Cummings.

3. Guiry, M. D., & Guiry, G. M. (2021). AlgaeBase. World-wide electronic publication, National University of Ireland, Galway. http://www.algaebase.org.

4. Huisman, J. M. (2018). Algae: An Introduction to Phycology. Cambridge University Press.

5. Larkum, A. W. D., Douglas, S. E., & Raven, J. A. (Eds.). (2012). Photosynthesis in algae. Springer.

6. Raven, J. A. (2013). Algae: Anatomy, Biochemistry, and Biotechnology. Springer.

7. Round, F. E., Chapman, D. J., & Maberly, S. C. (2014). The Ecology of Algae. Cambridge University Press.

8. Stewart, W. D. P., & Fitzgerald, G. P. (Eds.). (1980). Algae as Ecological Indicators. Academic Press.

9. Van der Meer, J. P. (Ed.). (2015). Handbook of Microalgal Culture: Applied Phycology and Biotechnology. John Wiley & Sons.

10. Watanabe, M. M., & Hattori, A. (2001). Algal Culture Collections around the World. National Institute for Environmental Studies.

ABOUT DAVID ALAN BINDER

David Alan Binder is a distinguished professional in the realms of editing, proofreading, assessment, and authorship. With an impressive array of credentials, he has garnered recognition as an accomplished freelance editor, proofreader, assessor, and esteemed author. Binder's literary expertise is highlighted by his publications which have earned him esteemed accolades, along with his extensive educational background and profound writing experience.

Education

- BS(Honors), Mount Mercy University
- Dean's List
- MPA, San Diego State University
- GPA: 3.4

Writing Experience

Notable Awards and Achievements:
- Beach Book Festival Award
- New England Book Festival Award
- Reading Life Award
- Astra Writing Contest Award
- Golden Wizard Book Prize
- Third place in the Children's Stories Anthology by Something Or Other Publishing

Literary Contributions:
- "The Manager's Manager: Strategies and Tactics for Effective Leadership"
- "Exploring Phycology or Algology: A Comprehensive Guide to Algae and their Significance"
- "Effects of Environmental Pollution on Properties"
- A captivating chapter book
- An anthology of children's stories
- Eight engaging children's picture books
- "An Anthology of Poetry: 1971 to Present"

With an impressive repertoire of writing achievements, David Alan Binder has proven himself as a skilled wordsmith, adept at crafting impactful narratives across various genres. His dedication to the art of writing is evident in the diversity and depth of his literary contributions.